*Here's what reviewers
are saying about*
TO HAVE AND TO HOLD

"At last a line that goes beyond the 'happily ever after' ending. . . . What really makes these books special is their view of marriage as an exciting, vibrant blossoming of love out of the courtship stage. Clichés such as the 'other woman' are avoided, as family backgrounds are beautifully interwoven with plot to create a very special romantic glow."
—Melinda Helfer, *Romantic Times*

"At last, a series of honest, convincing and delightfully reassuring stories about the joys of matrimonial love. Men and women who sometimes doubt that a happy marriage can be achieved should read these books."
—Vivien Jennings, *Boy Meets Girl*

"I am extremely impressed by the high quality of writing within this new line. Romance readers who have been screaming for stories of romance, sensuality, deep commitment and love will not want to miss this line. I feel that this line will become not only a favorite of mine but of the millions of romance readers."
—Terri Busch, *Heart Line*

**Today my husband is
coming home from prison
as a hero, and I'm
terrified . . . Chris thought.**

Outside, a car door slammed. Startled, alert, she heard footsteps on the concrete path, a key grinding in the front lock.

"Don't move," he said, and came to her, walking slowly, his gaze steady, holding her. Facing her, he rested his knee on the bench. Its hard warmth touched her thigh, igniting a sharp thrill in her senses. Only one man could do that to her and it was so good to see him, so good, that she wanted to fold him into her body. She started to tell him.

"Jesse . . ."

He gently touched his forefinger to her lips. "You don't have to tell me. Not now." The tip of his finger moved across her face, tracing her cheek. His gaze was luminous, almost wondering.

"Don't move, Chris," he whispered again. "I just want to look at you."

Dear Reader:

The event we've all been waiting for has finally arrived! The publishers of SECOND CHANCE AT LOVE are delighted to announce the arrival of TO HAVE AND TO HOLD. Here is the line of romances so many of you have been asking for. Here are the stories that take romance fiction into the thrilling new realm of married love.

TO HAVE AND TO HOLD is the first and only romance series that portrays the joys and heartaches of marriage. Its unique concept makes it significantly different from the other lines now available to you. It conforms to a standard of high quality set and maintained by SECOND CHANCE AT LOVE. And, of course, it offers all the compelling romance, exciting sensuality, and heartwarming entertainment you expect in your romance reading.

We think you'll love TO HAVE AND TO HOLD romances—and that you'll become the kind of loyal reader who is making SECOND CHANCE AT LOVE an ever-increasing success. Look for four TO HAVE AND TO HOLD romances in October and three each month thereafter, as well as six SECOND CHANCE AT LOVE romances each and every month. We hope you'll read and enjoy them all. And please keep your letters coming! Your opinion is of the utmost importance to us.

Warm wishes,

Ellen Edwards

Ellen Edwards
TO HAVE AND TO HOLD
The Berkley Publishing Group
200 Madison Avenue
New York, N.Y. 10016

THE TESTIMONY
ROBIN JAMES

SECOND CHANCE AT LOVE
BOOK

Thanks to Lois Walker; to Marcia Rachofsky;

to Carol Wahlen;

to Ted Kivitt of the Milwaukee Ballet

and to Joe,

who was an inspiration to us.

THE TESTIMONY

Copyright © 1983 by Robin James

Distributed by The Berkley Publishing Group

Special Preview Edition / June 1983
To Have and to Hold Edition / October 1983

First printing

Printed in the United States of America

To Have and to Hold books are published by
The Berkley Publishing Group
200 Madison Avenue, New York, NY 10016

This book is dedicated to Jane Coleman,
for contributions beyond value
over many years.

chapter one

She had loved Jesse Ludan for five years. Today, after six months away, he was coming home, to her home, to her bed.

The home was Victorian Gothic, a century-old residence of creamy brick with carved gables and stained glass in the transom windows. The bed, inherited from a locomotive engineer uncle of Jesse's, was a brass-framed antique that drank brass polish by the pint. She could put on dainty floral sheets and ruffled throw pillows and drape the frame with the granny-square comforter, but without Jesse the bed had all the comforts of sleeping on the cold stony ground.

The thought drowned in a surge of guilt. Jesse had been sleeping in a bed that was so much worse.

Christine sat alone, her feet curled against the ivory cushioned window bench that circled the interior of a

1

small Gothic turret beyond the living room. In the garden outside the bay window, a butterfly danced in the morning sunlight, its shadow fluttering through prismatic ribbons of light thrown on the warm cedar walls by the beveled window above. The ballet slipper she had picked up to mend lay in her idle fingers. Jesse's image filled her mind.

Jesse, I need you. I've missed you so. *Hurry*.

Again she tried to estimate how long it would be before he walked through the front door: the legal formalities, the visit—short, she hoped—with his lawyers; meeting with the waiting press; the ride home with his brother, who could be trusted to drop Jesse off and disappear. How long? It was impossible to tell. Late afternoon at the earliest, the lawyer had warned her.

Her shadow fell near the floating outline of the butterfly. Once, twice, it seemed to settle like a bow in her hair. Her hair—her mother had called it "that unfortunate red" in the same way she referred to the time Cousin Cecil broke his fingers in the power window of his Rolls-Royce as "that unfortunate incident with the foreign car." But Jesse would dip his fingers into her bright curls and spread them upon her pillow, whispering against her skin that each strand was like a streamer stolen from the setting sun.

When it came to that, her mercilessly freckled complexion was a good deal more unfortunate. Gay splotches of rioting melanin covered her everywhere, even the soft, secret, intimate places, which had made it painful for her to undress the first time she and Jesse had made love. Wonderful Jesse—he had been so tender that night, murmuring gently teasing encouragement, covering her—freckles and all—with slow, sensuous kisses that made her feel as though her body were a special miracle filled with delight, giving delight. But six months later, in the week before their wedding, she had asked him snappishly how he would be able to stand spending the rest of his life looking at a speckled body—the question resulting from a good case of prewedding jitters, the strain left in the aftermath of an argument with her mother, and a rather immature impulse toward self-punishment. And he had answered her with that exhilarating grin of his and said, "After you, I'm afraid a body without much color interest would seem a little tame." Laughing, he had dragged her against him, even though they were on the main thoroughfare of a shopping mall, and had whispered in her ear, "You don't believe I think you're beautiful? Come home with me and I'll spend every minute left in the day showing it."

Nice as it was to hear, she knew very well she was no beauty. The rigorous moves of classical ballet training are performed to a wall of mirrors. Every detail of her face and body was familiar to her; she had no illusions. The slight roundness of her jaw, the clear blue eyes, the straight brows, and the nose that had no qualms about tilting upward a bit at the tip gave her face, even at twenty-six, a Disney-kid look that the freckles did nothing to dispel. Bartenders still asked her for identification. In the desperate search for acceptance during her teens, she had even—horrors!—tried false eyelashes (they fell in the pizza at the sophomore dance) and bleaching her hair (her mother made an appointment for her with a psychoanalyst). There was, however, a certain expressive mobility to her face, and people seemed to notice her smile. From time to time, strangers had even crossed the room in public places to say that watching her had brightened their day, never knowing how much they had brightened hers by saying so. All her mirror ever showed her was freckles and the kind of face that begged to be chucked under the chin. People meeting her for the first time were inclined to think she was shy. She was inclined to think they were right.

Shy was, of course, the last adjective one would apply to Jesse. Jess could talk to anyone with ease. Or he could six months ago. Lately, in those too-short moments they were allowed to spend together on the telephone, he had sounded terse, at times even detached. Six months ago that quality had been as foreign to his character as California sunshine is to the pristine brilliance of a Wisconsin winter.

Jesse was a man involved with life. Milwaukee was his city and he knew every part of it. Christine had been born and shielded through childhood in the North Shore suburb of Fox Point, and to her the city to the south had seemed gray, industrial, and crime-ridden, a place entered cautiously to visit the theater, to drive through on the way to restaurants. The last thing she had ever expected was that she would marry a man who had grown up in the shadow of a Milwaukee brewery in a "rear house," one of the tiny homes built at the turn of the century by Eastern European immigrant families on the backs of their lots to shelter newly arriving relatives. Jesse was the second of twelve children whose parents had been forced to leave Hungary during the 1956 revolution. He and his brothers and sisters had been fed and clothed on their disabled father's Social Security check and the income their mother made cooking at a Catholic seminary. And probably the last woman Jesse had expected to marry was a neurosurgeon's slightly insecure daughter with a diploma in fine arts from Mills College and a trust fund from her grandmother.

The attraction between her and Jesse hadn't been instant and animal. Well, perhaps it had been a little animal on her part, but a painful crush or two in her adolescence had taught her not to toss her heart like a rose. Her smile notwithstanding, she had never been the sort of woman who drives men into a frenzy. She had assumed he would be conceited—who wouldn't have been with his bright caressing eyes, his soft thick layers of light-brown hair, his beautiful cheekbones, his body?

A strong, incalculable pull had kept them seeing each other for the two months it took for her to realize that he was softer and more sensitive than she might have guessed—and for him to realize that she was stronger and more open than her Orphan Annie freckles suggested. But her heart had raced ahead of her common sense. She had fallen in love with him a month before she could believe with any assurance that it was safe. By some unquestioned miracle, he had begun to love her in return.

He had come to mean so much to her, this man who could transform a meaningless gray day into a perfect pearl on an endless string. With him, she had changed from a person who faced her mirror image with a look of half-quizzical exasperation into one who could walk down State Street and kiss her fingers at her reflection in the shop windows.

During his absence, she had held his image like a jewel in her mind. Jesse in a tavern after a soccer victory, his team pouring beer on his head while he laughed. And later at home, Jesse heading toward the shower until she called him back, a delicate suggestion in her voice . . . watching him turn, smiling; watching him come toward her, his green eyes widening slightly as she tossed her T-shirt to the foot of the bed; and he, pulling his soccer shirt over his head, laying it with gentle deliberation over hers. The thin fabric of the briefly cut soccer shorts made him seem more uncovered to her than the innocence of nudity, and she could remember the long, elegant stretch of his legs with their golden sun color; and, above the teasing interruption of his shorts, the lighter gilded tone of his chest with its subtle pattern of muscle and baby-soft frost of hair.

And she could see him in the kitchen in a white cotton shirt with the sleeves rolled up, his arms plunged to the elbows in a sink full of dirty dishes, while she sat in a chair tending her flu. He came to her with a lacework of shining soap bubbles on his arms that transferred to her hair and skin as he caught her hot cheeks in his palms and pressed a light kiss on her lips. . . .

And then the picture would change to a late evening on the shore of Lake Michigan. Jesse in the calfskin bomber jacket she had given him for his birthday, the wind drifting it open to show the quilted lining, the Fair Isle sweater, the thin wool scarf, the narrow hips of his faded jeans. She could taste the tang of autumn and lake breeze on her lips and the fading warmth of a distant sun as he stretched down for a stone and gracefully sent it skipping into the darkening water. That was the night he told her he might have to leave her soon.

A hollow rumble came from the sidewalk in front of the house as a gang of small children rolled from the alley on their Big Wheels in a stampede of brightly colored plastic. The jewel image of Jesse faded. A quick upward glance toward the living room dragged Christine back to the present as she noticed the telephone receiver dangling glumly at the end of its short cord. "The Phone That Rang Too Often: A Moral Lesson." She had let it drop after the last call, saying, "Hang loose, phone." Jesse had said he wouldn't try to get through. She had already talked to everyone else who mattered; there was no risk. The last three days had brought a barrage of calls. The receiver would reach out to her with a fresh jangle as soon as she returned it to its cradle. News that Jesse might be coming home any time was spreading. Family called—his and hers. Friends called—his, hers, and theirs. People didn't mean for their concern to become harassment, but the sheer number of calls had become a relentless battering on her psyche.

As frequent were the calls from the press, the geyser of questions. When do you expect your husband, Mrs. Ludan? Have you talked to him? How does he feel? How do you feel, Mrs. Ludan? She had answered them in vacuous elegies to her joy until her tension had built so high that she knew she couldn't do it another time. Her phone—and her psyche—were both left dangling.

How do you feel, Mrs. Ludan? Terrified. Today my husband is coming home from prison as a hero, and I'm terrified. . . .

Her gaze refocused suddenly on her still hands, the curving fingers that held the poised needle, and she realized that she'd been deep inside herself, disconnected like the phone.

Outside, a loud motor was idling at the curb. A car door slammed. Startled, alert, she heard footsteps on the concrete path, a key grinding in the front lock. The door was opened and quietly shut. Quiet also were the footsteps that came forward, then hesitated.

"Christine?"

Jesse's voice. *Jesse's voice,* rich and soft and close, keenly real, shed of the telephone's electronic tinge.

"I'm back here!"

Quickly his footsteps began to retrace the path of her voice. Thoughts came to her like little sparks: breathless delight, sick longing, fear; and a silly dismay that here she was in a faded pink flannel nightgown with a scrubbed face when she had wanted to rifle her closet for something stunning, subdue her hair with a curling iron, put perfume and blusher on all the places on her body where *Cosmopolitan* insisted they ought to go—and do a hundred other things that wouldn't matter to him but to her were a love ritual.

Jesse stood in the frame of the arched doorway. Angled sunlight found his hair, lifting honey tones from the smooth minky layers. "Strokable hair," her sister had called it. His eyes held the beginnings of a smile, a soft glow that gave the irises the clear color of sun-filled birch leaves. The firm lips echoed his spare smile. She knew his face heart-wrenchingly well; yet as she gazed at him it seemed as though she had forgotten the sensuality of his features, the suggestion of sexuality that made women looking at him think of swift, unplanned seductions and lazy erotic aftermaths. In certain expressions his mouth had a sardonic tilt that had both alarmed and fascinated her in their early acquaintance; she had been sure he was silently mocking her. But then he had smiled at her, an open smile of such startling charm that she remembered wondering if her spirit would burst from its fast trip upward. This smile was different. It was raw.

He had allowed his hair to grow in prison. In back it covered his collar, and that burned into her again the feeling that too much time had passed since they had been together. Under the heather-gray blazer, the ivory cotton shirt, the soft wool pants, she knew every exquisite play of skin and muscle, every dense curve of bone and tendon. She knew them, but for six months she hadn't had access to them.

"Don't move," he said, and came to her, walking slowly, his gaze steady, holding her. Facing her, he rested his knee on the bench. Its hard warmth touched her thigh, igniting a sharp thrill in her senses. Only one man could do that to her and it was so good to see him, so good, that she wanted to fold him into her body. She started to tell him.

"Jesse . . ."

He gently touched his forefinger to her lips. "You don't have to tell me. Not now." The tip of his finger moved across her face, tracing her cheek. His gaze was luminous, almost wondering.

"Don't move, Chris," he whispered again. "I just want to look at you."

Yet his eyes closed for a moment as his palms molded themselves to the contours of her face. His thumbs delicately outlined her eyebrows, her lashes, her eyelids; they followed the shape of her lips, and then, more playfully, the down slope of her nose, softly tilting the tip upward. One hand curled under her throat urged her chin up, and then his eyes opened into the love in hers.

She felt his full interest as though it were a material presence hovering near the edge of her thoughts, absorbing signals and clues. It was this slow gaze that had always made her want to save a hundred details from each day to tell him in the evening—and there had been six months of days. But now the urgency to speak had

faded as he seemed to draw the dark loneliness from
her—through her flesh, into his hands, into his heart.
His love stroked her, soothing a sore place within her.

His palms moved slowly lower, warmly enclosing the
sides of her throat, his thumbs offering a careful support
for her chin. There was a stillness about him, a concen-
tration that seemed more intense than anything she could
remember. It was almost as though he couldn't believe
she was there. Even as she reveled in his emotion, it
awed her. His thoughts were far from clear to her, but
she felt the weight of them. His name was a murmur on
her lips as her arms traveled the achingly pleasurable
path around his waist and she buried her face in his
stomach. Tears came, cooling the slight roughness of the
fabric, as his hand made long slow passages over her
hair.

The lilting chime of the doorbell pealed through the
room, and she awoke to the sound like a dreamer, uncertain what had aroused her.

A curiously passionless frown crossed Jesse's face. It
was a numb expression, unreadable. He was quiet for a
moment, his hands in a light embrace on her shoulders.
The bell chimed again. He let his hands fall away and
said in a mild tone, "Were you expecting someone?"

Her fear returned. Not *we. You,* he had said, like a
casual visitor who would be leaving soon, leaving her
alone with her doorbell, her life. Six months. Had she
expected him to flow back into their life together as easily
as if he'd stepped out to the corner store for milk? No.
But being without him had been so hard that she wanted
it to stop being hard now.

"I told everyone not to come," she said, and felt a
second twinge. Would he read condescension in that?

Would he read control? For six months the rigid prison structure had controlled Jesse's every move. "That is— I really wanted it to be just us today. I hope you don't mind." She was frustrated by her tone; it seemed defensive, babbling. She tried to correct it. "Your family wanted to come, but they seemed to understand, and I . . ." The bell rang a third time, its deliberately pretty chime taking on an abrasive edge. She stood quickly to answer it, to spare him the vexation. Then she thought, My God, that *is* condescending. She forced a smile. "Would you like to get it?"

He gave her a curious look and turned, his gaze traveling to the unseated telephone. "What's been going on? Has someone been bothering you? The press?" His tone was curt, shot with coiled animosity.

They had been bothering her but she didn't want to tell him. This was Jesse—her husband, her lover—and seven months ago she would have given him all her thoughts as though they belonged to him as much as they did to her. As their ordeal began, her feeble efforts to protect him in small ways had been useless. But even now she lied.

"Never. I count them as family." She walked into the living room, with its light-colored dhurries, its airy patterned wall coverings, and chintz love seats. Padding barefoot across the oak floor to peek out through the louvered shutters, she continued, "Speaking of which, it's channel twelve—I recognize the Action News van. Oh, and there's Harrison P. Fosdick, complete with capped teeth. And he's wearing a trenchcoat."

"After the manner of Bernstein off to interview Deep Throat." Jesse's voice came from just over her shoulder. "Is it only Harry?"

She looked again. "No. There's another car pulling up with that young guy from the wire service. Ben..."

Jesse's lips carried the ghost of a smile. "Mittman. Let's drop hot oil on them from the battlements. Remind me sometime to find an honest way of making a living. Christine?" His expression had become soft and searching. He took her hand. "You look terrified. Someone hasn't been taking very good care of you for six months."

Her gaze met and held his in a moment of sparkling sweetness. "Don't worry about me," she said softly. "Take care of yourself. When you're all right, I'm all right."

Solace bloomed in the light-green eyes. He lifted her hand, slowly spread her fingers, and kissed her palm. "Then I'll try extra hard to be all right." Releasing her, he started toward the front door, but halted as though some fleeting, potent thought had touched him. He turned. "Straighten my tie."

He wasn't wearing one. Christine felt her heart quicken. It was a long-standing joke between them, something to cling to, a symbol that said lightness was not a thing they would let disappear from their lives. In mime, she studied the absent tie with the formality of a valet, made infinitesimal adjustments to the knot-that-wasn't-there, tugged fussily on his collar, and flicked invisible particles of lint from his jacket. Standing back with one eye closed, the other eyebrow in an exaggerated arch, she viewed her handiwork over an upraised thumb, like an artiste. "Nah, wait a minute." She reached up, grinning, to rumple his hair. In a tone that suggested she was immensely pleased with herself, she said, "There," and kissed her fingers to his tousled hair.

Instead of flashing the answering smile she had expected, he pulled her into his arms and held her tightly, whispering something into her hair that was too low for her to catch. After a moment he left her, without speaking again, to face his media colleagues waiting outside. Christine sat down on the couch, trying to rub the headache from her temples and the leftover tears from her eyes. When that failed, she climbed the creaking oak stairs to the bathroom and scrubbed her face. As she flipped through her closet, randomly dragging clothes from hangers, she discovered that her hands were shaking.

She dressed in a shetland crew-neck sweater, a shirt, and wool slacks, then decided they made her look as if she'd stepped out of the pages of a preppie handbook. *Gag me with a spoon*. The clothes came off in a heap. She eyed the Ralph Lauren suit her mother had brought back for her from New York. No. Every press report of Jesse's case referred to her as his "wealthy socialite wife." The last thing she wanted to do was reinforce that image. Not only was it patently untrue, but it made her feel like the kind of strange social category that college freshmen studied in survey courses—the Luddites, the Hittites, the Socialites. When the *Chicago Daily Post* covered Jesse's case, their reporter had misread the wire service rip, and she had been mentioned as his wealthy social*ist* wife. Jesse had burst out laughing and then written the *Post* a scathing letter in protest. Personally, she was convinced that somewhere in the steamy depths of Washington, D.C., her name was now on file in an FBI office.

Going outside, finally dressed in a long gray sweater that was ruffled around the neckline and a comfortably long wool voile skirt, Christine found their small front lawn busier than feeding time at the zoo. Television videotape cameras nosed around near the front door, their short proboscises poking curiously here and there like rooting aardvarks. Reporters milled, chatting to Jesse and to one another with the gossipy intimacy of confederates. Not, of course, that they wouldn't have run one another into a ditch to get the scoop on a story, but they were obviously feeling a little silly about interviewing one of their own kind. Neighbors were beginning to appear, descending the steep front lawns of hefty Revival-style houses. Those who considered themselves too sophisticated to stare made themselves busy raking leaves or taking swipes at their winter-ravaged hedges with clippers.

Not the Crosbys. A husband and wife team of attorneys, they lived directly across the street and drove the house-proud of the neighborhood into a frenzy by refusing to mow their lawn, under the sardonic claim that they were letting it return to prairie. Just now they were set up on the sidewalk in lawn chairs to watch the goings-on, with stadium blankets, binoculars, and scotch. They saluted Christine gaily with their glasses when they caught her wave and shouted, "It's a happening!" Their kids were putting up a lemonade stand.

With the panting vigor of two sheep dogs, the young Action News cameraman and Harrison P. Fosdick herded Jesse from the mob. The cameraman stopped to inspect the dial of the pack underneath his arm.

"There isn't much charge left in these batteries," he said.

Fosdick frowned. "You should have checked that before we left. Oh, for the days of film..."

"When men were men," Jesse murmured.

"Beg pardon?" said Fosdick, turning.

"Nothing." Jesse smiled. "I'm ready whenever."

"Thanks. I'm gonna ask you to sit tight for a second here while I put in my intro." Fosdick threw Jesse a curiously glazed smile and bared his teeth at the cameraman. "There had better be juice enough in that pack of yours for this interview." Stationing himself about ten feet from the camera, Fosdick shook out the microphone cable and clipped the tiny cylindrical mike to his lapel. Straightening, he scowled, then nodded to the cameraman, then gazed sincerely into the camera. He began to walk forward, speaking in a booming baritone.

"It is to this quiet East Side Milwaukee neighborhood that journalist Jesse Ludan returned today a free man. Jailed six months ago . . . ah, *shit.*" He'd tripped on the cable, sending the mike leaping downward to bounce off the top of one of his wing-tipped oxfords. He swept it up, glaring fiercely, and caught the grin Jesse wasn't tactful enough to hide. "You print guys don't have to worry about this stuff," he chided, reestablishing himself in front of the camera and becoming sincere again. "Okay." A pause.

"It is to this quiet East Side Milwaukee neighborhood that journalist Jesse Ludan returns today a free man. Jailed six months ago for refusing to give testimony before a John Doe investigation of an antinuclear demonstration last summer, Ludan and his case have become a cause célèbre, drawing international support and media attention . . ."

Christine heard the words, but she was watching Jesse's face, remembering the nights she had carried grocery bags full of letters to Jesse's parents' house. They and his brothers had sat with her around the kitchen table wreathed in the warmth of their wood-burning stove as they tore open envelopes and wrote answers until two o'clock in the morning. Not everything that came in the mailbox had been friendly. Some disagreed politely. Some were derisive. Some were much worse. Jesse's mother had said wasn't it a shame that there were such twisted people in the world, and Jesse's older brother Sandor began to insist on screening her mail. None of them had revealed any of this to Jesse, though he often asked. There would have been nothing for him to do about it but go insane with worry.

Media attention. There had been a network clip she had never seen of Jesse's father and her father escorting her from the courthouse on the day Jesse was jailed, her face white and streaked with the silver weave of falling tears, her eyes shut in pain. . . .

Jesse, speaking to the camera, was saying, "There's nothing complex about the issue. The components of a free press are reporters who aren't afraid to tell a story and citizens who aren't afraid to talk to reporters. If things people say to the press can become criminal evidence against them, people are going to learn not to talk to the press."

Fosdick leaned closer in a listening posture. "Could you explain why you think criminals have the right to that kind of shield?"

"Could you explain why, in a nation that assumes innocence until conviction, you would stick a label like 'criminal' on people who've never been convicted of a crime?" Jesse snapped with such sudden impatience that Fosdick's head jerked back in surprise. "If you understand the Constitution, you'll understand that I went to jail to defend innocent men and women, not criminals."

Disregarding the microphone—Christine suspected he was going to feed this little incident into the tape eraser anyway—Fosdick said curtly, "That's semantics, Ludan."

"Is it? Too damn bad you don't know the difference between semantics and principles." But as soon as the words left him, his expression began to change, and Christine felt her heart contract as she saw his surprise mirror Fosdick's. She watched the man she loved as he brought his hand to his forehead and closed his eyes, rubbing gently. She knew the gesture. It meant utter exhaustion. The busy front yard grew quiet, alert with mute interest.

Jesse lifted a palm toward Fosdick. "Harry . . ."

With wary sympathy, Fosdick forestalled explanation or apology. "Hey, forget it, pal. Now that I know what kind of hand we're playing, I'll deal 'em easy, okay? Are you willing to give it another shot?"

Jesse dropped his hand and looked around, his light-green eyes searching until they found and settled on Christine. His shoulders relaxed and he turned a strained smile back to Fosdick and nodded.

Several others had followed the direction of Jesse's gaze to where Christine stood in the shadowed overhang of the porch. One gave his camera a suggestive boost.

"Chrissie!" the cameraman called. "I didn't see you hiding up there. Come on down and let us get some shots of you and Jesse in a happy clinch." He laughed at the strongly negative shake of her head. "Still camera-shy, eh? Well, I'd still rather expose a few feet of tape on your pretty face than Jesse's any day of the week."

Stray male compliments embarrassed her, but rigorous early training from her mother had taught her never to deny them.

"They call me the Mo Dean of the civil disobedience circuit," she said.

"Modine. Isn't that a town in Illinois?" Fosdick's eyes widened perplexedly, spider monkey style.

"That's Moline," someone said. That drew laughter, then more banter, and questions for her and for Jesse, who had retreated into calm, concise answers. It was all in the line of duty. If you went to jail for six months, you sure as heck wanted to make people understand why, even if you were so tense you could hardly unfreeze your mouth to speak. As soon as Christine could, she said she heard the phone and escaped into the house.

She tried to give it half an hour—in the line of duty. But in fifteen minutes her resolution snapped, tumbling silently around her like a broken kite string. She went back into the front yard to tell Jesse in a perfectly normal voice that his father was on the phone. He nodded, said, "Excuse me" to the clustered journalists, and followed her back inside with long strides. He picked up the receiver and listened to the dial tone. His eyes held amusement and light curiosity as they strayed to Christine's face.

"It's the bee," she said, answering his unspoken question. The bee: their private idiom for the dial tone's hum.

He smiled slowly and set down the phone. "It's not going to work, you know. They'll camp on the sidewalk, and hide in the garbage cans—"

"—their beady eyes peering out of the darkness from under the lids," Christine finished. "My fault. Indy offered to come and talk to them so we wouldn't have to face them today, but I thought... I don't know, that you'd talk to them on the courthouse steps or something."

"*My* fault. I ought to have the emotional ballast to evict them gracefully." His right hand found her shoulder, his fingers working their way through the warm curtain of her hair, curving softly around the back of her neck. His gaze touched her eyelashes, her lips, the light play of color in her cheeks. Without breaking contact, he stretched one arm down, cradled the receiver, and dialed four numbers.

She dropped her head back into the slow massage of his fingers. Pleasure pulsed through her shoulders and fanned through her throat, spreading downward, tightening her nerves. Jesse spoke into the phone.

"Could you give me the number of the Wisconsin Ballet Company, please? Thanks." He dialed again. "Yes. I'd like to speak to Indy Ludan, please.... Yes, I know that, and I'm sorry about the interruption but..."

The steady stirring movements worked upward, tracing her spine and then dropping, slipping open the single button that closed her sweater.

"Tell him it's his brother. Right. Jesse. Thank you very much, I'm glad to be home too. Sure, I'd appreciate that. I'll hold."

The fingers moved under her sweater and impelled her slightly forward until she could feel his body against her. Her thin skirt permitted the firm impression of his hips. Her chest cushioned achingly against his. The open lapels of his jacket fell in a teasing pressure on the sides of her breasts. Throughout her body, dormant neurons began to awaken, to search out the familiar print of his hard contours, the stretch of his thighs, the linear symmetry of his ribs.

Jesse's conversation with his brother was short. Dropping the phone on the hook, he said, "Indy's on his way. Lord knows what he's going to tell them."

"Glib stuff," she started to say, but the phone and the doorbell rang together, the two sounds bitingly out of pitch. Though his body remained motionless, she could feel the tension that ran through his muscles. "We don't have to stay in here, do we? Let's escape," she said.

He understood her instantly. "Out the back? Let's go."

A bubble of exhilaration rose in her as he grabbed her hand and ran with her through the house, out the back door.

The back garden breathed color. A gardener for the county park system had owned the house before them, and his plantings smiled on. Massed tulips grew straight and tall in shades of gold, cherry-red, and lemon-yellow with a band of creamy white. Tiny lilac-pink bells of wood hyacinths pealed in sweet, silent harmonies under the melodies of songbirds. Fresh grass threw upward the wet loamy fragrance of spring and silenced the faint sound of their running feet.

White picket fences, or hedges not fully in leaf, separated the pretty string of backyards. Two fences away a red station wagon with the logo of a radio station on its front door was driving slowly down the side street. The driver saw them, made a sharp stop, shouted a greeting out the window, and gunned the wagon in reverse, heading toward the alley that lined the backyards where the garages formed neat, unpretentious rows.

Jesse stopped. "The goblins are circling. That's Angela Currie."

She knew. That face she could recognize at five hundred feet because she'd seen it so often in the past gazing invitingly into her husband's green eyes. Angela was young, talented, glowing with personality, and had the tenacity of a pit bull.

"Jarochs are gone," Christine offered, glancing at the surgically neat yard next door.

"Do you want to make a break for it? Let's bust out of this joint. The jailbreak of my dreams." He put himself neatly over the picket fence into the Jarochs' backyard and held out his arms to her. "C'mon over the big wall. Watch out for the searchlights—the bulls may have a piece trained on us. My, oh, my!" he said, watching her hitch her skirt up and prepare to leap into his arms. "This is more fun than I expected."

His hands caught her at the waist and lifted her, and, because she was a dancer, she knew how to make that easy for him. For six months there had been no Jesse to lift her over hurdles, to tease, to tempt, to laugh with. The unhealed residue of that stark emptiness clustered in her chest while her body swept his fleetingly. He settled her before him with care. Pain and the fluttery pleasure of his closeness rippled together, and she wanted only to feel his love, to have him fold himself around her like a mist and consume the memories of her suffering. And in some ways his smile did that as he pulled her into the sanctuary of the Jarochs' lilac bush.

"Jesse?" Angela's too-musical soprano came from behind them. The back gate creaked sharply in their own garden. "Oh, Mr. *Lu*-dan..." In an undertone, "Well, damn it, where did he go?" The high heels reached their patio and continued off around the corner of the house toward the front, tapping a demanding tone on the antique bricks.

Christine took one look at Jesse crouching beside her,

his face haloed by lilac leaves, and they collapsed against each other in silent laughter, caught like children in an electric moment of total irresponsibility.

"That woman is trespassing," Christine whispered.

"We should call a cop. If they throw her in jail, *I* can do a story on *her*. Are you sure the Jarochs aren't home?"

"Positive. They left for the lake this morning. Would I have entered this sacred preserve else?" She put a hand on his arm, correcting a small dip in her balance.

"Right. Or he'd try to force us to borrow his fertilizer spreader. Look, it ill befits our dignity to hide here under a bush. Instead I think we should hide in the toolshed. Do they still keep the key over the door frame?"

With exaggerated stealth, they crept to the Jarochs' small outbuilding and let themselves furtively inside, tiptoeing like cartoon burglars. Gasping with laughter, bent over the doorknob, she said, "This is *so* immature."

But Jesse had stopped laughing. He stood against the wall near the coil of a green garden hose, eyelids lowered, his cheekbones a sharp statement in a remote countenance, as though all stimuli had suddenly become a burden. Then he opened his eyes and brushed his hand briefly down her cheek.

"Thanks." His tone was quiet, his half smile made with effort.

Effort also made her answer light. "For what? Skulking through the shrubbery like an idiot? For you, kid, anything." No. No. This wasn't Jesse—the lapses of mood, the flares of temper. Her mind rebelled, rejecting it. The stress of prison, the swift transition from bars to media stardom to home—she must be crazy to put him under a microscope today of all days. Easy, Chris. Love him. Just love him.

She took a sustaining breath. The air was slightly musty, scented of warm wood and the chemical tang of solvents that clung to the neat row of paintbrushes hanging on a pegboard. Lawn tools, ladders, and leaf baskets hunched against the walls at stiff attention, as if afraid they were about to be reviewed by a marine drill sergeant. A high window projected a square of ivory sunlight on the back wall.

Jesse stepped on a short ladder and pushed open the window, flooding her flushed skin with cool clean air. Climbing down, he bumped a narrow shelf and a spool of fishing line rolled to the cement floor, tossing off yards of thin curls. He bent absently to retrieve it and began to walk back and forth in the small room, his steps automatic, almost unconscious. Pacing. He was pacing. She had seen wild creatures do the same thing in circus cages. Had he learned it in prison, the unthinking defense of an animal to the agony of confinement? A body fighting to maintain its precious store of health, circulation, muscle tone, coordination?

There had been too much to absorb at first, so she had missed it. His proportions had always been beautiful and long, and spliced together in an easy way that gave his body a coltish grace. Somehow in prison he had managed to lose a few pounds, and the missing weight added a certain ranginess to the flowing lines of his frame, indefinably accenting his sensual bone structure. It made a delicate alteration in his appearance that was strange to her.

There were other changes too, less tangible ones. He had always possessed that sort of charismatic animation that in women people tended to call vivacity. She could only imagine what a burden that energy must have imposed on him in prison. Here was the product: vitality too long checked had become nervous tension, as a powerful engine left in neutral will idle restlessly.

She could no longer stop her mind from its merciless analysis. No thoughts rose to comfort her. Only anguish came like a cold knife pressing into her stomach. What have they done to you, Jesse? What have they done?

chapter two

Jesse became aware all at once that he was not talking, and that Christine was resting against a sawhorse, staring at him. Silence had become a natural condition for him; he had slipped into it as easily as he breathed. He had discovered how to erase thought, so that it became possible to pass hours in a state of white blankness impenetrable to sound and light and the passage of time. As the months passed he had used the skill more often. At first it had been only a tool to fight boredom, which had never been something he'd handled well. But later it became a shield against the crushing claustrophobia, when the sheer tonnage of walls and bars closed over him. In a thousand lifetimes he would never forget that moment this morning when he had stepped outside into air that was fresh and sweet and tinged with city smells, the scents of human activity.

Prison air was dense. It had an unventilated feel of too many men drawing oxygen from the same depleted source. Odors of food and cleaning fluids never escaped. They clung like wraiths to walls and skin and clothing. The shed's thick air had been too potently evocative, and a trapped feeling had begun to descend upon him, as though he were lying in the path of some vast gear that was grinding slowly closer. He had steadied himself and opened the window—calmly, he hoped—and then, as he began to walk, the steady motion had seemed to define and throw open space. The claustrophobia had evaporated, and with it, his thoughts. Withdrawal had become a habit. Happy news.

He wanted to bathe. Lord, he wanted to bathe, but Indy wouldn't have had time to arrive yet and politely repel the representatives of a fascinated public. They had allowed him to shower that morning, a favor since it was off hours; but that had been prison water and it seemed to stain as it cleansed. It occurred to him to wonder if he smelled. A certain bitter amusement accompanied the speculation, and he glanced back at Christine and saw that her eyes were wide. His silence had frightened her.

Don't, love. You don't have to be afraid. I love you, Chris. That part of me will never alter. And the rest will touch you as little as I can make it possible.

"Maybe I saw the garden at a run, but it looked beautiful. You must have been working hard." He chose the subject at random. The work went into making his voice natural and his expression light. Her urchin's smile was his reward.

"Mr. Jaroch didn't think so. He vaulted the fence last month and trimmed the yew hedge. Kinda tossed the cut branches down in disgust, so I guess I didn't get to it soon enough."

"Are you kidding? I suppose that's what you'd expect from a guy who crawls around his lawn on his stomach pulling crabgrass sprouts out with tweezers."

"The Jarochs do have a terrific lawn."

He dismissed this piece of fair-mindedness with, "Big hairy deal."

"Big hairy deal?" Her grin was off center.

"Right." The lazy stretch of his arm captured a bright curl, and he cupped it against his palm while using his forefinger to brush the soft crease that cornered her smile. Her cheek tilted to rub a kitten's caress on his hand, and somehow that simple gesture, so typically Christine, so free from calculation, brought a good hard knot to his throat. Six months. Six precious months of his life with her were lost and never on this earth would they be restored. He had a sudden acute struggle to keep his feelings from expressing themselves in the way he had been taught from childhood was not permissible for a man.

"Jess?" Her blue eyes had grown solemn.

"What, love?"

"I don't know how to ask this . . . Jesse, I don't want to blast things out of you that you're not ready to talk about but I have to know . . ." An uncertain pause. "How much haven't you told me? Was prison . . . was it horrible?"

Was it horrible? she had asked him. There she stood in her silk knit sweater, her Gucci shoes, and one of the expensive skirts she wore that clung, but never too tightly, to her slender thighs, asking him if prison was horrible.

Her eyes were serious and bright with the fetching sincerity that seemed like such a poor defense against the ~~darker aspects of life and that, paradoxically,~~ always made him want to bare his soul to that uncallused sanity. The soft taut skin over her nose and cheeks shone slightly in the highly filtered light, paling her freckles, giving a fragility to her face with its combined suggestion of sturdiness and sensitivity. He would have thought four years of marriage might have banished any unease he felt about what a sociologist would label the "class difference" of their backgrounds, yet looking at her now, he had never felt it more strongly.

He'd had his own nose rubbed firmly in reality at a young age because there were plenty of things about his tough South Side neighborhood that his Hungarian immigrant parents never realized. But the woman he loved had been raised in the exclusive womb of upper-middle-class America, sailing not always blithely but certainly securely from the house with the white pillars and circular driveway to the academically prestigious private school, to dinners at the country club and private dancing lessons. Indy had said once that Chris had learned everything she knew about life from watching television talk shows, and there was probably a certain cruel truth in that. Prison was alien to her—thank God. Everything she knew about it came from the carefully preselected things he'd told her in their short telephone conversations, when there had always been some other poor sucker waiting desperately for a turn. Where else? Sources like photo essays in mass-market newsmagazines, well-meaning but aseptic, their choice not innocent of aesthetic considerations. They could tell you how a prison looked, but they could never touch the smallest part of what it was like to live inside one.

Was there a line that stopped somewhere between caring for someone and taking care of her? If shielding Christine was patronizing or arrogant, he couldn't help it.

There was a reel of fishing line in his right hand. Where had it come from? The window shelf. He let her thick curl slide from his fingers and walked slowly to the shelf, reaching up to replace the roll, letting the motion hide his face while he spoke.

"It was a little horrible." He leaned his back against the workbench, gripping the edge. Gently shifting the focus away from himself, he said, "Was it a little horrible here without me?"

"It was a lot horrible here without you." The admission seemed to relieve some of her tension. "Not that I'm proud of being so dependent on a man, mind you."

"Say three Our Fathers, two Hail Marys, and read six months of back issues of *Ms* magazine. Go in peace, Daughter, and sin no more." He gestured a blessing. Then, putting a palm lightly over his own heart, he added, "I had the same thing. Desolation."

"You missed the daily dose of me?"

"I missed the daily dose of you."

Her toes turned inward, freckled fingers threaded anxiously together. The round chin dropped and she gazed at him from under her lashes, a mime of bashfulness.

"So here we are—alone at last," she breathed.

Sometimes mime was a game for Christine, sometimes a refuge. In college she had joined a small troupe that passed a hat in the city parks. To combat her shyness, she still used it, retreating as though to the anonymity of whiteface and costume.

He could feel the anxiety pent up in her. *Show me you're all right, Jesse.* Something elemental in his life seemed to hinge on his comforting her. He searched desperately for the self he had been before prison, trying to clone the person she would know and recognize and feel safe with.

"Alone, and in such romantic surroundings," he said, taking a step toward her. His heel touched a shovel blade, sending a shiver of reaction through the nervously perched lawn implements that lined the wall. Some interesting quirk of physics kept them upright except for one rake that came whacking to the floor at his feet. "Ah, the hazards of these secret liaisons! We've got to stop meeting like this—the gardener is beginning to suspect."

"The gardener I can handle, but when a man in his prime is nearly cut down by a rake..."

"A *dangerous* rake." His voice lowered. "This, my dear, is Milwaukee's most notorious rake. More women have surrendered their virtue to him than to the legions of Caesar." He lifted the rake tines upward and made it walk toward her, giving it a lascivious whisper. "Don't fight it, *cara*. Your body was made for love. With me you can experience the fullness of your womanhood."

She laughed at his notion of the things rakes say, garnered three years ago from a teasing thumb-through of a certain deliciously fat romance novel that she had meant to keep better hidden. Raising one hand dramatically to ward off the rake, she said, "Leaf me alone, lecher!"

The rake took an offended dip and marched back to the wall in a huff. "Reject me if you must," it said in a wounded tone, "but must I endure a bad pun about my honorable profession? I thought women were supposed to love a rake," it added hopefully.

A smile hovered near the edge of her husband's mobile lips. Christine recognized a certain quality in it that made her heart beat harder. As his hands came lightly down on her shoulders, her lips parted without her will and her gaze traveled up to meet the shadow play of desire in his eyes.

"Some women prefer their very own husbands." There was a slight breathless quiver in her voice, and the throb of tightening pressure in her lungs.

"Hot damn. A compliment." Jesse let his thumbs slide down the front of her shoulders, rotating them with gentle sensuality over the soft flesh that lay above the rise of her breasts. She had begun to tremble under the sure movements of his fingers, and her slipping control brought back to him all the warm nights they had shared, the tangled sheets, the pungent musky air. He remembered the rosy flush of her upraised nipples and the way they felt on his lips. . . .

It had been so long, more than six months, since they had been together, six months since he had even seen a woman. He wondered if she realized that, or guessed how her nearness made his senses skyrocket. He wanted her to give up her body to him, to offer herself to him like an expanding breath for him to touch and taste and fill, to watch her bluebell eyes grow smoky with rapture. But though he drew her close so that he could feel the lovely fullness of her small breasts pressing into his ribs, he made no move to lower his hands or to take her lips. She seemed entrancingly clean, like a just-bathed child, and as pure. The damaged part of him came to her almost as a supplicant, unwhole before her wholesomeness. Can I touch you, love? Tell me it's all right...

She couldn't have heard his thoughts, or seen them, because he had learned too well to disguise them; yet her hands came to him like an answer, her fingers entwined behind his neck, pulling him toward her warm mouth. He took a breath as her lips skimmed over his, and another much harder one as she stood on her toes to heighten the contact. Her tongue probed shyly at his lips and then forced an entrance, her body twisting slowly into his, a sinuous shock against his thighs.

He murmured something, random words of desire he couldn't remember as he said them; the pressure of her lips increased, and he felt thought begin to leave, and a growing pressure behind his eyelids. His hands were drifting over her blindly, as in a vision, until a shuddering fever ran through his veins and he dragged her close, pulling her hard into him, holding her there with one arm while the other slid under her sweater, his fingers spreading over the powdery softness of her skin. A surprised moan swept from her mouth into his lips as his hand lightly covered her breast. His palm absorbed her warmth, her delicate shape, and the thrillingly uneven pattern of her respiration before slipping to the fine heat and velvet distension of her nipple.

This time he heard his own whisper, the unchosen words coming in huskily slurred Hungarian, telling her that he loved her, that she bewitched him, and then repeating her name again and again with the rhythm of his mouth and tongue. He was overcome, lost in her elemental femaleness, his pulse hammering through his body. Leaning her back, bringing his mouth hard against hers, he poured his kiss into her until their rapid breathing came together and he could feel every silken inch of her with the front of his body.

A keen breeze rattled the roof of the shed. It might have been the sound that brought him back, or perhaps some inner thermostat of his own, but he became aware suddenly that he was going to take her here in old man Jaroch's toolshed. And then he thought, Oh, Christ, how hard have I been holding her? His own muscles ached from the force, and he brought his head up to examine her upturned face. Sleepy lashes dusted her cheeks. A contented smile curved over damp and swollen lips. Her skin was lustrous. He pulled her into the curve of his arm with a relieved sigh, cradling her while he tried to contain his overwhelming appetite. Not here, Ludan. Not like this, with half your mind on freeze.

Kissing her once on each eyelid, he steeled his self-restraint and put her very gently from him. Her eyes flew open; her gaze leaped curiously to his.

"Heart of my heart, I'm sorry," he said softly, smiling at her, "but if I don't take my shameless hands off you . . ."

"I might end up experiencing the fullness of my womanhood in a toolshed?" she finished for him. Her returning grin had a sexy sweetness that tested his resolution. "It's not the worst idea I've ever heard."

But it is, Chris, he thought. Because enough of me hasn't walked out of that cell yet to make what would happen between us into an act of love. And the trust I see in your eyes would never allow me to give you less.

chapter three

The sun was a silver blaze in a dense sky when Christine awoke the next morning. The newspaper said that it was an atmospheric condition caused by forest fires in Canada. The spring had been dry, but in a few days the breeze would wash the residue to the east and the sun would shine on Wisconsin again. Maybe. Forest fires. Drought. Other natural disasters. Jesse hadn't come to bed with her last night.

The sheets had the cool, unnourished feel that a body alone can give a double bed. If he had been with her, she would have known, even in sleep, and treasured it.

There was no evidence to show where Jesse had slept. The spare bed hadn't been touched. There were no hastily folded blankets stuffed in the cedar chest to implicate the living room sofa, though he had sat there to read. Several books—his—lay on the glass side table. She picked them up, handling the worn bindings lovingly. She studied the title pages: Sándor Petöfi, Attila József. Hungarian poets. All she really knew about them was that Petöfi was a national hero who fought to liberate the serfs and died in battle in the nineteenth century at the age of twenty-six; Jesse's older brother was named after him. József was a revolutionary who wasn't many years older when he committed suicide by throwing himself under a train. Jesse would have winced at that characterization. He would have said it would be like calling Abraham Lincoln a Civil War-era party boss who was shot in a theater.

She stared down at the pages, frustrated by their incomprehensibility to her. They were words written by idealists, men like Jesse. But Jesse said that English translations of Hungarian poetry were pretty much useless, and a working knowledge of Hungarian wasn't just around the corner. In four years of marriage all she had picked up were scattered phrases. Hungarian didn't hail from the Indo-European family of languages, which meant that the words weren't cousins to English. Jesse frequently tried to tell her Hungarian was easy because the words were pronounced phonetically, with no grammatical genders. Possibly. But their alphabet had about forty letters, give or take a few letter combinations. The transitive verbs had complicated conjugations. It used postpositions instead of prepositions. And the words that stared innocently up at her were so complex that their own mother wouldn't have recognized them. She set down the book.

In the kitchen she found a note. "Chris: I'm off to the paper. There's an omelet mix ready for you in the refrigerator. U R my"—and he had drawn a small smiling sun.

The sun notwithstanding, there was little illumination there. That he'd gone back to work immediately was no surprise. From the beginning he had said that he would, and the stubborn gesture was so characteristic of Jesse that she had never doubted he would carry it through. In a way she could understand the need to quickly reestablish the normal course of his life. It might even have something to do with replenishing the self-esteem that must have been draining away with icy certainty while he was imprisoned. That fear alone had stilled the fierce protests she would otherwise have made.

Not that he would get anything resembling work done today. At the paper, Jesse would be met with the same cannonade of support and awe that had kept him on the telephone from the moment he had stepped into their house from the Jarochs' toolshed. No, that wasn't right. He had showered first, for an inordinately long time, and she remembered how it had made her smile. It must have felt good to spend as much time in the shower as he wanted to again. After that . . . how could he refuse to talk to his father, or to his editor who had stood behind him, or to his godfather who called long distance from Houston? And then the call from his close high school friend—who had become a priest and ran an inner city rehabilitation program for derelicts; and the call from his favorite professor at the University of Wisconsin. The list went on. He had been on the phone when she went to bed at nine-thirty assuming he would join her soon. She'd had little rest in the past week, since it had begun to look like this time rumor didn't lie, that the John Doe investigation was finally winding up and the judge would have to order Jesse's release. Sleep had come to her quickly, but it was the light, uneasy span of drifting consciousness that had been her nighttime companion for the last twenty-five weeks.

The lump in her stomach didn't want the omelet. But she ate it anyway because he'd made it, and she had as many sentimental idiocies as any other woman in love. If she'd had tears left, she would have cried them. Why hadn't he slept with her? Making love with Jesse made heaven inside her. She needed that feeling. She had depended on its irresistible sweetness to begin reweaving the severed threads, the faint too-tiny-to-be-seen rent in the marriage fabric that time and tension and pride had left behind. That Jesse hadn't felt the same need to be with her came as a body blow.

Not having been blessed with Jesse's zeal for stomping through trouble in hip boots, she had canceled classes at her small ballet school. But the empty day rose before her, a sterile wilderness of inhospitable hours. Jesse would be late coming home. He was stopping off after work to visit his parents, who, to be fair, had also missed him desperately. Between phone calls he had tried to talk her into coming with him, but his cramped family home with its gauntlet of alert, knowing faces was better faced later.

A survey of her closet yielded a lavender sweater. She pulled it over her head in front of the bathroom mirror. The cowl neck looked like it was trying to swallow her head. She wasted ten minutes trying to subdue it, then thankfully noticed it had a moth hole. The moth— friend of man. She was going to raise them and train them to eat all her clothes-purchase errors. The little devils had avoided her new Ralph Lauren suit. Possibly a glance at the price tag had given them indigestion.

She threw on the suit quickly before she could change her mind, arranging the dainty ecru folds of the lace scarf at her throat, opening the front-buttoning skirt to her knees. Watching the stern Donegal tweed flare over her legs, she did a couple of poses she'd seen in *Vogue*. Feet apart, hands on hips, pout at the mirror. It was the kind of outfit that begged to be postured in, and it carried the typical hazard of all haute couture—she wasn't sure whether it made her look great or grotesque.

In a city as big as Milwaukee there was no need to be lonely. She knew a number of people who would have been sympathetic company; friendly, reassuring people. Instead she was going to see Jesse's brother Indy.

Indiana Ludan was easy to find. But that was the only thing about the man that was easy. Any belief that arrogant, promiscuous men were traced with a romantic aura could be cured by an acquaintance with Indy. She had seen the scars he'd left on his deserted lovers.

The scents at the Wisconsin Ballet Company were richly evocative—cologne, cigarettes, sweat, damp clothing, and Ben-Gay. Walking into the barnlike vastness of the rehearsal room she picked Indy out at once. He was alone—the unapproachable star. He lay on the floor at rest, his arms open and relaxed, his feet crossed at the ankles and thrust upraised against the sunny creaminess of a high brick wall. A shaft of steamy light dropped through a frosted window, softening the outline of his body. Blood-red leg warmers concealed his legs, but sweat had plastered his body-hugging orange T-shirt to his torso, revealing every justly famed inch. Little diamonds of perspiration glinted in his hair.

A group of leotarded dancers from the corps de ballet

clustered around a distant piano, the graceful images multiplied by the mirrors that covered three walls. One girl was coaxing an inexpert version of "Ragtime" from the keyboard. The rest slugged down canned cola and candy bars while standing balanced on one leg, the other leg in *passé* or touching one sharply pointed toe to the floor in postures reminiscent of exotic water birds resting with long-legged ease in the shallows. They glanced curiously at Christine as she crossed the wide floor, then returned to quietly chatting.

Indy's eyes were closed, a signal that he probably wanted to be left undisturbed.

"Looks like you're into some heavy relaxation," she said finally.

Haunting heavy eyes opened slowly. The long mouth developed a soft Byronic twist. In a light movement, his arms came to pillow the back of his head, the gesture intimate and unconsciously sensuous. He must have been surprised to see her. She only saw him in family groups and had certainly never sought him out. But the jaded temper didn't easily reveal surprise.

"They're thinking of installing a television in the ceiling so I'll keep awake during breaks watching *General Hospital*." Moss-green eyes regarded her steadily. "Why did you drop by, dear?"

It was a fair question. She had come because, arrogant cynic though he might be, Indiana was more than Jesse's brother; he was Jesse's best friend. No one in the world understood her husband better. But he was hardly an easy confidant, and the direct inquiry made her hedge.

"I had an errand in the neighborhood and I thought I'd drop in to thank you for helping us out yesterday."

His smile dawned briefly. "Bull." He slanted himself

onto one elbow. "Have lunch with me, and we'll talk. I have to miss class this afternoon. The chiropractor's going to work on my back at two-thirty." With tender mockery, he added, "You're a frail flower, Chris. I command you to stay alive while I change."

He returned in a dusky-rose crew-neck sweater, impeccable suede pants, and the black beret he seemed to wear for the sole purpose of bugging his father, who called it "that damned pancake thing."

The wind was brisk. Gusts from Lake Michigan blew through the crooked canals that led downtown, teasing up Christine's skirt and throwing Indy's honey-blond hair into a skipping dance as they crossed a drawbridge. Sailboats moored in a narrow channel rustled in the breeze under white gulls mewing in motionless flight through a cool faded sky. The heart of the city rose around them, prettily archaic. Streamlined modern structures were a rare and fragile species here, as though the modernists had thrown up their hands in defeat and gone off to build in Los Angeles. No one came to Wisconsin to crane his neck at skyscrapers. Christine often heard it said that Milwaukee had a downtown impressive for a city half its size.

Ballet fans in the noontime crowd of secretaries and executives turned to stare at Indy. They had reason. At nineteen he had been the young phenomenon, the protégé who became a principal danseur at one of the world's greatest ballet companies, in New York City, where East Coast critics hailed him breathlessly as the finest young dancer in America. Heady stuff. Four years later, at the peak of his public adulation, he had left New York abruptly to dance in Milwaukee, which, as far as the East Coast media establishment was concerned, was like dancing nowhere. Balletomanes struck their collective brow in horror. Few people beyond the family knew about the phone call from Manhattan that had put Jesse on the next plane to New York, or about the cocaine addiction that had almost destroyed the country's hottest ballet star. Fame was not all joy.

Christine had met Indy once, very briefly, at the height of his reign when he had guest lectured at her college. With a smile and a wince she could recall how she had gawked, and pumped his hand, and gushed into the vacuum of his polite boredom. And then, with eighteen-year-old impetuosity, she had made much more of it than there was to her friend Marilyn, never anticipating that in two years she and Marilyn would see Indiana Ludan at a lakefront jazz festival, or that Marilyn would grip her arm with maniacal strength and drag her cringingly forward to renew the supposed friendship. Indy had no idea who she was, and wasn't the kind who troubled to pretend, but the man with the perceptive smile at Indy's side had been Jesse. And what had happened in that mortifying episode to amuse him and interest him in her, Christine had never quite understood. Jesse just said he was a sucker for terrified women.

A puff of lake-scented air tossed her lace scarf, and Indy's fingers smoothed it back into place. "Mama's been on another pilgrimage to the Big Apple?" he said. "You realize, don't you, that there are only three people in Milwaukee who'll know that's a Ralph Lauren. In the Midwest you get better value for your status dollar by putting it into a car."

"Or tearing out the backyard for a swimming pool. You know what? I'm in a masochistic mood. Tell me how I look. I'm too short to wear this, right? Rate me.

Scale of one through ten—be brutal if you have to."

"A tempting offer. I'm more interested in what's going on inside than outside, but if you'd open three more buttons on that skirt, I'd give you . . . maybe an eight and three quarters. Let's talk about this masochistic mood of yours."

She had meant the remark as a joke. Echoed back, it became oddly telling. To avoid his eyes, she glanced sideways toward a construction site wedged between two hotels in the style Jesse had taught her to recognize as Victorian Italianate. There a crew of hard hats were eating pastrami sandwiches. One of them caught sight of Indy, nudged the guy beside him, and said through a mouthful of rye, "Hey, look, Harry—a French guy."

Crinkling smile lines wreathed the corners of Indy's pleased grin. When they stopped at the light, he draped an arm over her shoulder, buddy style, his hand dangling gracefully.

"What troubles your heart, my little cabbage?" he said with a French accent.

Doubts and vague images of her betrayal fanned from her conscience. For this first time she meant to break faith with Jesse, to unveil a fear in her marriage to an outsider before she shared it with Jesse. Pride and guilt made her hesitate as the traffic signal ordered them to walk and she stepped down with him into the street.

"Could you kind of wheedle it out of me, do you think?" she asked.

"I thought I was." His fingers crept up to give the fat gold hoop of her earring a gentle tug. "Should we take out from Watts' and eat in the park?"

"Brilliant! But are you going to give me trouble about having dessert?"

"Of course not. Why would I care?"

"That's what I'd like to know. Every time I put on an extra pound, you pinch it and say, 'What's this?'"

"I've never done that!"

"Oh, ho ho. You certainly have."

They had arrived at the Watts' Building, two stories of ornate Moorish designs worked in a terra-cotta facing. Downstairs the Watts family sold fine china. She and Indy tiptoed, bickering, between glass racks of Wedgwood to reach the elevators to the tearoom upstairs, where waitresses in black with white lace aprons served fresh-faced brides come to choose their china patterns, and charming ladies with blue-white hair and mink stoles. Once she had brought Jesse and he had counted ten minks and refused to come again.

Outside again, peppy breezes scattered paper in swirls around their feet as they found a stone bench and unloaded lunch in a park full of pigeons, whispering trees, and flying spray from a wide round fountain. Taking cautious sips from a steaming paper cup, Christine said, "Here's your coffee. This one's my Russian chocolate. Have you found my ginger toast? Oh, thanks. What does it say on the little sugar packages?"

"Trivia questions." He flipped his over and read: "Who played the wealthy society lady in the Marx brothers movies?"

"Tiny Tim?"

Flipping over the package, he said, "Sorry. Margaret Dumont."

She drew one of her own from the brown paper bag. "You realize, of course, that this means war. Who sang 'Ol' Man River' in the original production of *Show Boat?*"

"Jules Bledsoe."

He was right. Even trivia was beyond her today. "That does it," she said. "The only recourse for my ego will be popping open three more buttons in my skirt to go from drab to dynamite. Think I should zip into a phone booth to do it?"

He had been warming his hands on his coffee cup, staring half-absently ahead. Suddenly his austere features resolved themselves into a smile. "Do it for Jess—you'll drive him crazy."

She froze. Randomly innocent, the remark lit her anxiety like a flare. She had to bite back the urge to fish for reassurance with a blurted denial. *If I can't talk about it without whining, I'll hate myself later.* . . . Her fingers felt ineptly heavy as she pried at the lid of her chocolate. A sense of her own failure spread inside her, her mistakes pounding numbly at her brain.

If I'd gone to see Jesse in prison, we would know each other now, she thought. But he had refused to let her come. She saw herself again the day of Jesse's hearing, each detail vivid as she waited beyond the closed courtroom in the hallway of pressed stone and barrel-vaulted ceilings, which were made more somber by old brass fixtures. Four hours; and then Jesse's lawyer had come through the heavy wood-paneled door with the words everyone but Christine had been expecting. The judge had ordered Jesse to be confined without bail until such time as the investigation was completed. The investigation could continue for a year. There had been no time for Jesse to scrawl a note. His message for her had been conveyed through the lawyer: *I love you. Please go home and wait for me to call. There's a chance I'll have access to a phone in the afternoon.*

It was later, on the phone, that he had told her not to

come. The words had been gentle, but cloaked in the force of an iron will. "We've got the phone, Chris, and we've got letters. Don't let the dire words from the judge scare you, love. I'll be out of here in much less than a year—maybe in a couple of weeks. I don't want you to worry. I'm pretty comfortable. In fact, it's been interesting. My only problem is thinking about what this is doing to you, and it'll help if I know you're safe and warm with the home fires burning."

The streak of protectiveness in his request had violated every principle they had established in their marriage. The argument that followed led to Jesse saying in a strained sigh made metallic by the telephone, "Don't come, Chris. I love you too much to expose you to this place."

After a moment of suffocated fury she had screamed back, "I don't want to be loved that much!" In the ensuing quiet of that first night, cold with shame, she had gone to bed with those words. She had never again fought with him on the phone. He had lost all liberty, all power now. Let him at least be able to have his choice in this.

It had begun. They were guarding each other. From then on their shields stood between them. Barriers. Boundaries. Too late, she knew she should have stifled the shame and kept the fury.

Aloud she said, "Did Jesse talk about me yesterday?"

Indy bit off half a strawberry and finished it before answering. "Anything juicy, I assume you mean? You know he doesn't do that, Chris."

"Not anything juicy. Anything."

She had never before tried to pump him about his private conversations with Jesse. The fact that she had the nerve and the need today must have begun to communicate her desperation because he said, "Only that the whole thing has been hard on you, and that makes him feel like hell."

"And you said . . . ?"

"That yes, it had been hard on you, but that you were a spunky lady and you were fine."

"Yes, damn it! I'm fine, Jesse's fine, everyone's fine! Except that no one is fine." Her wrist smacked her knee, interrupting a vigorous gesture, and hot chocolate slopped from the cup, stinging her hand, wetting the dusty cement at her feet. His fingers came quickly to remove the cup and blot her hand with a napkin before he seized both her hands in an aggressive grip.

"You're scaring me, Chris. No more stalling. What happened last night?"

Feeling sick, she said, "Jesse didn't come to bed with me."

He released her cramped fingers. "Are you talking about sex or sleep?"

"Both."

"Did you have a fight?"

"No. It's probably too soon to panic, but this has never happened before. . . . Indiana, tell me not to panic. Something's wrong. I can feel it. He's been hurt. God knows what they could have done to him in there that we don't know about. Terrible things can happen to men in prison. I saw a special on channel four last week that said—"

"It doesn't matter what you saw. If Jesse was raped in prison, he would have told you, no question. He's no eighteen-year-old kid. There are things too serious to play around with. Smaller stuff he might try to carry on his own. That one, never."

The words, clear and measured, described Jesse to a finite edge. Indy was absolutely right. Christine tried to discover her relief, but all she found was the thought, *What smaller stuff?* revolving like a pinwheel through her disorganized mind. All at once she was hideously embarrassed by her emotionalism, by her hysterical imaginings, by her inability to cope alone with the intricate stress of Jesse's release. What had been panic dropped abruptly into quiet depression and frustration with her myriad inadequacies. Her hand shaped itself around her brow and then dropped lightly to her knee.

"Of course. Why am I being so stupid? Jess and I just need time. I'm sorry I bothered you, Indy. Look, I'm not really hungry. I had a late breakfast, so if you don't mind, I think I'll let you get back to—" It humiliated her to end her sentence midway, but she had no choice. Her voice was breaking. She had begun to rise. His hand on her arm stopped her.

"Can I put my arms around you?" His voice was soft, gentle, as she had never heard it before, and it made her furious.

"No! I'm not eighteen either. I won't be babied."

The silence was awkward, and she could feel in it the reflection of her own helplessness, because he had come to fully understand, as she had, that he lived in symbiosis with Jesse's strength of character. And even the strongest of human beings have a terrible fragility not seen or thought about until something stabs out, testing: Fate as predator.

"I'm in the advice market." Emotion sandpapered her voice. "I'll take anything. Cheap shots. Barroom psychology. Aesop's fables . . ."

A pause. "How about one cheap shot and an allegory?" He handed her another napkin for her nose, seem-

ing to examine her silent assent. "Don't try to be so
wonderful. It's not invisible—that effort. Since Jesse
went in, the family has watched you barter little pieces
of yourself as if you were trying to get so perfect that
someone floating around in the clouds would look down
and say, 'That's one hell of a nice little girl down there.
Let's not mess around with her life anymore.' But that's
not how it's going to work. If you keep it up, you're
going to come apart like a picture puzzle."

Some marginal parameter of her brain noticed that the
chocolate left in her cup was shaking. "I said cheap shots
accepted, not thoracic surgery."

"Sorry. I'm not good at saying things gently. You
asked for help: I'm doing my best. Listen a minute. About
five summers ago I danced at an outdoor festival in Canada. Natasha Churbanova and I were doing the wedding
bit from *Sleeping Beauty*. It was hot and muggy and
mosquitoes were eating the hell out of us, and that made
everyone nice and tense. When I held Natasha, I could
feel her body trembling like a wet puppy's. Her leg was
hurting her. But everyone dances hurt, right? That's ballet—body abuse. That night in front of a full house she
went up on pointe. All of a sudden there was this loud
crack. You could hear it all the way back to the cheap
seats. Her Achilles' tendon had snapped; you could see
it curling up like a scroll on the back of her leg under
the skin. They had her into surgery within the hour so
they could get to the thing before it atrophied. The point
is, you should never ignore a sore Achilles' tendon."

Feeling vaguely harrowed, she said, "How long did
it take her to recover?"

"Two years, the doctors said. But she was dancing

again in six months and onstage again in nine. You'll turn it around, Christine. But don't try to buy Jesse's sanity by sacrificing your own."

"Be plain, please."

"If you want him in bed, dear, then you ought to tell him."

She swiveled to face him, cold chocolate in hand, cold anger inside. "Just how selfish do you think I am? After the pressure he's been under, I should insist on a big performance in bed?"

The long mouth stretched up at one corner. The dusk-green eyes began at her face and traveled over her in a slow survey, a thorough, infuriating, and very gratifying salve to her tottering confidence.

"There's not a single doubt in my mind," he said, "that the poor, poor man will survive the torture."

chapter four

Jesse Ludan didn't get a lick of work done all day. For one thing, he had become a hero and everyone from the printers to the publisher wanted to wring his hand. It meant nothing to him, because he had fallen into the role almost by accident, and because he had always despised reporters as celebrities—it was so damned hypocritical. But mainly he kept those reflections to himself. When he voiced them, people tended to come away saying he was modest, and that irritated him more than all the rest of it put together. It was better to keep your mouth shut and be a little misunderstood than to open it and be misunderstood totally.

In a quiet moment after an overly effusive and hail-fellow heavily alcoholic lunch at the press club, he had gone to his desk and dug out the column that had put him behind bars. It was a competent little piece, not one of his best. When one writes for a living, one turns out a lot of drivel. Editors with a deadline needed words to fill the paper's news hole; words had to be there whether the muse came or not. Jesse didn't mind. It was worth it for the occasional white-lightning high of writing something he really felt, and knowing that the next afternoon a whole county of people were going to stare at it, and get angry or happy, depending on their philosophical bents. He was controversial; the city wasp putting a sting to all shades of the political spectrum. His favorite memories came from the times he walked unknown into a tavern and watched it come alive with an argument over one of his columns, men and women howling their viewpoints, brains working at fifty miles an hour, tongues at a hundred. He had thought, That's right, this is a democracy. Revel in it.

His post-high-school involvements with women had been mostly with political activists. Christine was not political. She tended to view activists as people who were always on their way to somewhere else, to a brighter, more beautiful world. Chris never saw the earth as a place filled with complex issues; she saw it as a place filled with complex people and simple issues. Her tolerance was far greater than his; it was one of the things he loved about her. He'd had many reasons in the last six months to be thankful for that quality.

The nuclear power plant had been a hot issue from the beginning. The power company had had the deplorable lack of tack to decide they ought to build the damn thing on Jones Island, a narrow peninsula that jutted out from the center of Milwaukee into Lake Michigan. Nice choice. Even with a huge public relations campaign about "our friend, the atom," there were any number of home folks who looked on the situation as over-my-dead-body-you're-going-to-erect-that-holocaust-maker-in-my-back-yard.

He was the only journalist the demonstrators had invited to that fateful sunrise vigil they held at the Jones Island construction site. Some people are just born lucky. So he had rolled out of Christine's warm arms on a Sunday morning, resisting the considerable urge to stay and turn her disappointed sigh into something husky and wanton. He had stood in the misty cold at six A.M., warming his hands in his jeans pockets during a short dawn rally, taking no notes, just watching the men and women who had assembled at the lonely site at an hour when most people were still in bed.

They weren't all strangers. Far from it. He saw the daughter of a coworker; an old girl friend of his brother Peter's; nuns from a South Side parish. When someone told him that construction equipment on the site had been sabotaged, his first reaction had been, Oh, Lord, why me? Why am I the sad sack reporter who has to hear this? You nice sincere people are going to end up in jail, and so, perhaps, am I.

He had written the article anyway—a mood piece, nothing polemical, just lyrical. He let the story tell itself except for a brief aside on the irony of how easily the powerful and expensive bulldozers and cranes could be demobilized—sand and sugar in the fuel tanks, distributor caps and injectors pulled. There were those who later interpreted that as an antitechnology stance, in the sense that a power plant was a machine, machines break down, we can't afford to put our trust in one fueled by anything as potentially devastating as nuclear energy. It was hard to remember now whether that was what he'd meant. Probably not. Who bothered being that clever at eight o'clock on a Sunday morning?

Predictably enough, the power company had had no sense of humor about paying for engine overhauls on their earth-moving equipment, feeling that, damn it, if they were so magnanimous as to build a nuclear power plant to supply the city with electricity, John Q. Public should stop complaining and count his blessings. You don't tug on Superman's cape, you don't spit into the wind, and you don't mess around with the power company. Not much time went by before the district attorney had a John Doe investigation going to gather evidence for charges of conspiracy to damage private property against the leaders of the antinuclear coalition. When his editor, Phil Jackson, found out who they'd pulled as a judge, he'd called Jesse and said, "I think we've got trouble."

Besides writing his weekly column of personal opinion, Jesse was a by-line reporter with a court beat, and this particular judge had been the disgruntled subject of one of his columns. Presiding over a case where a young woman had been sexually assaulted in her backyard, the judge had lectured the victim about mowing the grass in her halter top. The go-for-the-throat tone of Jesse's resultant article had been influenced more than a little by the fact that, when Christine mowed the grass, she often wore her halter top.

Sure enough, a month after the investigation began, they had slapped him with a subpoena. They wanted the names of the people he'd seen at the sunrise vigil, and all he could hope for was that when he refused to cough up, they wouldn't want to make an issue of it by ordering him confined to jail. But with an aggressive DA who was pushing for a promotion to head of the Felony Unit, and a judge who was likely to be voted out of office next election due in part to a Jesse Ludan column, things didn't look rosy.

He had tried to prepare Christine, but judges to her were white-haired gentlemen with twinkling eyes who played golf with Dad. They didn't put nice people in jail for being in the wrong place at the right time. Furthermore, this was the United States, and everyone had a right to a trial by his peers. Secret tribunals couldn't order people willy-nilly into jail. And if the judge tried anything, they'd appeal all the way to the Supreme Court if they had to. When he'd tried to explain that under Wisconsin statute 972.08 (2), secret tribunals *could* order people willy-nilly into jail, that an appeal would take five years to reach the Supreme Court and would probably lose, and that the Constitution had been interpreted to provide surprisingly flimsy protection to journalists under these circumstances, she had looked at him as though he were some kind of Bolshevik. She might have been more ready to face the coming ordeal if he had forced her to accept the nasty reality, but he hadn't had the heart to batter through that frail shell of optimism. In the month before he testified, when everyone was admiring Christine's courage, he knew that her poise came from an inner conviction that he wasn't going to jail, and that knowledge still made his heart twist.

He had never considered cooperating with the John Doe, because he'd been raised to believe that questions of conscience were not matters of choice. In any number of countries around the world, it was suckers like himself who made up the statistics for Amnesty International. And if he'd ever managed to slide around his ethics, how in heaven could he hand over information that would put a pair of nuns in jail? He visualized them staring mournfully out from their cells in their habits, penguins behind bars. The good Catholic education his parents had beggared themselves to provide had never made him devout, but for God's sake, *nuns*. . . .

That evening he spent with his family, rehashing the lighter points of the last six months, reassuring his grandmother that no, he hadn't picked up head lice, American prisons were very clean; and being good-natured when his mother stuffed him with about three times as many *kürtös kalács* as he wanted, under the touchingly misguided notion that he had spent the six months in jail pining for Hungarian pastry. Love kept back the confession that he would much rather have had a Big Mac.

He needed to be home with Christine, but he hadn't even begun to slough off the disturbing sensation that he had become an alien invader in her immaculate universe. The fear was strangely untouchable, encased in some sort of obdurate covering that resisted his efforts at penetration.

He said good night earlier than they were ready to part with him, knowing they would understand, but when his brothers Sandy and Peter walked him to his car and produced three bottles of Hungarian wine, he was uptight enough about his own lack of mental well-being to say "Sure" when Peter suggested they go to his apartment to drink it. Indiana joined them at the last minute, and, having a car full of his brothers, listening to their familiar banter, slipping into the easy particular pattern of his sibling role, Jesse found that he had begun to feel more real and less like an escapee, driving over the freeway under the pale spring moon.

Then his rearview mirror framed a police car with its cherry-red dome flashing. A shadowy impulse, hardly acknowledged but still present, pricked him to flee, to stop and get out and run. He had a sudden icy awareness of the three wine bottles Sandy was holding in the front seat, of the apricot brandy his father had served him, of the Baggie of grass that was probably in Peter's coat pocket. And when the police car sped past, intent on some other subject, he pulled to the shoulder and sat with his face pressed into the steering wheel. Afterward, Sandy drove.

Jesse made it home by ten-thirty and relatively sober, which was something of a feat, given that Sandy's solicitude had expressed itself in his plying him with vintage wine. Christine hadn't wanted to join him at Peter's; when he'd phoned to ask, she'd told him cheerfully that she "had things to do." She'd sounded like she meant it, though under the circumstances that much nobility was a little out of character. She was practicing self-denial to give him the freedom he needed to reassemble himself. He had been able to give her nothing in return except perhaps the restraint in holding back as much of the pitching of his sense of identity as possible.

Last night had been a blur, spent trying to experience his freedom, to believe in it. Small things had become luxuries. He drifted from room to room, looking at familiar remnants of himself—the wall of books in English and Hungarian, the record racks where his Smokey Robinson nested with Christine's Bach, the drawers of clothes that seemed wonderfully soft and fragrant after the prison coveralls that had corroded his skin. It's over, he kept telling himself. It's over.

Last he had gone to their bedroom, drenched in bliss, as though it were a gift he had been waiting to open. Christine had lain asleep in a square of moonlight, her moppet's hair tousled and dark against the pillow, her hands folded in prayer fashion under her cheek like a child in an Edwardian lithograph. She stirred. The falling cover bared one smooth leg, but he killed the quick response of his body as though it were profane. With his own heart beating a silent rhythm in his throat, he had studied the small exposed ear, the delicate sharpness of her thin shoulder, the pearly translucence of her flesh. He didn't want to be in bed; didn't want to close his eyes and lose himself in sleep. He had stayed awake watching her, getting up sometimes to wander the house restlessly, to end up finally in the big easy chair in the living room alternately dozing and waking with a start, the scents of his own home forcing him awake with the power of their reality.

Jesse put the car into the garage and came up the back path through the moist fragrance of her flower garden. One light shone in the second story behind the curtains. He let himself in the rear door. The living room lay in feathery darkness. Flat surfaces caught invisible light in pale waxy accents, cooling the black shadows, and from the partly open bedroom door a soft glow, warm and inviting, spilled down the stairs toward him. Something made him follow the beckoning path of light, two steps at a time. Outside the door he hesitated, trying without total success to force down the nagging sense that he was an intruder here, and then he pushed the door with the touch of one hand.

Christine sat on the bed in a mist of candlelight, straightbacked and cross-legged, and barely covered in a diaphanous body-skimming topaz nightgown. Another woman might have struck an erotic pose. But Christine sat perfectly still, looking back at him. When realization came, it hit him like a brickbat.

Every inch, *every* inch of the brass bed frame she had covered with flowing yellow ribbons.

Christine had watched Jesse enter the room and freeze. His eyes, bright as a Halloween cat's, held hers in an unwavering scrutiny, but whether he approved, disapproved, or was shocked she couldn't tell. Stubborn inside, she scrambled to her knees, knotted an imaginary lariat, twirled it expertly overhead, and lassoed Jesse. She tugged. He stood transfixed. She tugged again.

Wistfully stern, and a little nonplussed, she said, "Are you going to come along quietly or am I going to have to muss you up, bub?"

His reply was soft. "If I come, will you promise to muss me up anyway?" The love inside him was painfully strong. It ached in his throat, behind his eyes, deep within his chest. Desire had returned also, the strong low swell of wanting her that he could neither leash nor deny. Part of him felt as bright and weightless as a flame, but his yearning for the comfort he knew her body would give him was a dark, turbulent presence that had slipped beyond his control.

She was a dim, golden vision and he moved toward her slowly, feeding his anticipation. Her eyes seemed to

open wider; a bond that delicately mixed love and desire
was pulling them together. She seemed perfect to him,
and perfectly desirable, the source and fulfillment of his
dreams. Before he reached her, he could feel the taste
and warmth of her.

Beside the bed he offered her his hand, because words
wouldn't come. Her fingers entwined with his, empha-
sizing the satiny delicacy of hers, the strength of his, the
brilliant accent of their wedding rings. His other hand
flexed slightly to fit the modeling of her cheek, and with
hypnotic tenderness his lips skimmed her brow and the
velvet folds of her ear.

"Thank you." His voice was uneven. "I think you
might be saving my life."

Resting one knee on the bed, he withdrew his hand.
In easy movements that belied the passion welling within
him, he picked up pillows from the cedar chest beside
the bed and piled them beside her. Then, with a gentle
grip on her shoulders, he nestled her back to half-recline
against them.

"Welcome home, Jess." Her breath was quick, almost
frightened.

"Christine, *édesem* . . ." He hardly knew the soft whisper as his own, nor recognized that he had translated
the endearment into his first language. Christine, my
sweetness, he had said. . . . "Make me feel it, *édesem*. I
need you."

"And I need you." She flushed and began to smile.
"My heart is racing."

"Show me."

She didn't remove her gaze from his face as she drew
him to the bed until he sat with his worn denim jeans
brushing her unclad thigh. She carried his hand to her

body, pressing his palm to her tearing heartbeat. The upper curve of his hand barely teased the tender weight of her breast, and her eyelids closed and then drifted slowly open at the heavy spur of pleasure.

He bent closer, bringing his lips to the place she had laid his hand. Soft kisses explored the slippery fabric, the hot contours beneath. Nuzzling, he buried his face in the undercurve of her breast, feeling her chest jerk sharply as she absorbed a dry breath.

"Oh, yes, love. Show me," he whispered, letting his lips move swiftly lower in a rough traverse of her ribs, her belly, slipping his hand under her, spreading his fingers low on her back, lifting her into him.

He wanted to prolong each burning caress, to imprint it deeply on his senses, but the ecstasy of being close to her was so rich that he felt unable to reach its deepest import. He wanted to stop each second mid-beat and ride inside its open ellipse for eternity, and he had to fight back the tidal wave of sensation that was dragging him toward an immediate deep possession of her.

He lifted his head, smiling crookedly with hazed vision into her overbright eyes. "I'm an open fire, dearest love. God knows what you must be thinking..."

"Jesse, it's the same for me." Her laugh had a captivating huskiness. "What have I been doing for six months? Gnawing the bedpost..." With fluent grace she began to edge apart the buttons of his shirt cuffs, and he shuddered as her fingers swept against his skin.

"If you could go to my cell block and look at bed five, you'd see an iron bedstead reduced to a pile of slivers," he said, not thinking about, not knowing how enchanting he was to her in his intoxicated passion. His palm curved a second time over her wildly beating heart and held there under her breast, making for her a warm, safe area of sensation as she took off his jacket. For a moment she dropped her face into the jacket's scarlet lining, inhaling the minty scent of the leather and of him.

But with a slow intense smile that made a tingling weakness spread through her legs, he pushed the jacket lower and gently freed the first button of her nightgown. Drawing apart the bodice, he placed his parted lips on the valley between her breasts and tasted the milky soft-ness with his tongue. Then he drew back and slowly found and freed the second button, and his lips lightly touched and rested above her navel. The stroke of his uncovered arms against her skin left tiny hot and cold shivers in its wake, and when he began to play a massage of openmouthed kisses over her belly and feather her skin with his tongue, his hand dropped to her inner thigh and found the pulse there with his thumb, stirring over it in a slow circle.

He answered her low whimper of desire, whispering against her skin, "You taste like sunshine. I can feel you all through my body, Christine . . ."

The glossy nightgown fell away from her, and her skin glistened in the candlelight, the freckles dappling her like pollen across a cherry blossom.

"Gilt-tipped ivory," he murmured, lifting his lips to hers, his hand never leaving its easy voluptuous motion inside her thigh. His other hand cupped under her neck, lightly kneading the smooth softness of her as his head descended to capture her mouth, pressing into it. After a clingingly soft beginning, his lips parted over hers. His tongue tipped the inside of her lips, and then entered her deeply. Her fingers, unsteady, dissatisfied, hasty, laid his shirt the rest of the way open, and the light abrasion of his fleecy chest hair against her aroused nipples shot ice-hot eroticism spiraling through her flooding nerve streams.

"Jess..." she murmured weakly as he roamed over her inner thigh with his fingertips and over her throat with his mouth. "It's been a while. You may have forgotten... you have to take off your pants."

So he was kissing her, laughing at the same time, shrugging out of his shirt, his shoes, the rest, and then more gently freeing her from the bikini pants of her nightgown. And then he lowered his head to her breast, riding the tip softly with his lips, relearning its distended beauty.

"You're so warm for me—I need you to warm me, Chris. I've been so cold." His mouth made blind, fevered trails over her body, capturing pulse points in her temples, her throat, stroking his tongue over the inside of her elbow.

In a shaken whisper, she answered, "I've been so empty, Jesse. I—" Her breath stopped as his hand began a lazy tracery of the hollow inside her thigh and then entered her and, with unerring gentleness, found her clitoris. Hot convulsions rippled through her limbs and she gasped out, "Jess—"

The sensitive fingers shifted, relieving the intensity. In a husky soft whisper, breathing painfully, he said, "Too much electricity, Chrissie? Is this better? Yes? Oh, love, you feel so good, oh, love. Say that you love me, Chris."

"I love you," she breathed. "I've been so empty, Jess. I need you to—" She paused, gathering oxygen. "I need you to fill me."

His hand dove into her frothy curls, gripping her,

pulling her toward his mouth, and their lips met in a long, deep, driving kiss. Tiny gasps rose in her throat as his lips tore at hers, and the aching need in each panting respiration was a welcoming call to the dark heat within him. Her eyes looked brilliantly blue, centered by dark love-opened pupils, her lips wet and parted, her breath coming rapidly, the rhythm broken by his touch inside her. He had stopped thinking, not by conscious choice but because his love-need for her had carried him to a plane beyond thought. For this moment, he experienced the total release from care he desperately needed. With his eyes closed, with her liquid desire shimmering on his lips, sustaining their kiss, he brought himself into her body.

The penetration was not easy. But he knew that only dimly. Nor did he really grasp her quivering tension. All he knew was the euphoric rapture of her softness, her tightness closing around him. Her trembling arms wound about his shoulders and she held on to him hard. Moving with downy lightness, his hands began to cover her, to trace her features, her breasts, her lower stomach, her buttocks, the backs of her thighs; but the exploration reached his brain as one word—Christine. My love. Dimly again, he realized that she had relaxed against him, that their bodies had become a single pulse. She filled his mind like honeyed cream. She was a mist of pretty dappled colors to him, like a winsome autumn day. His voice whispered scattered passion words, sex words, to her, but he could not hear them—it was the rushing voice of his love, as natural as a waterfall.

He was breathing in soft rhythmic murmurs that mingled with her own, her exhalations stroking his lips like a warm breeze. His desire was a pounding thing, searingly hot, stripped of everything but the sweetness of her, feeling her sleek body beneath him, the smooth damp flesh over lean fine muscle, with exquisite curves and hollows that seemed made for the fit of his lips and tongue. They were as one body—as if their search for spiritual union had worked a strange medieval magic, recreating them as one soul. He gathered her face to him and brought his mouth back to hers in a last nourishing kiss, and the meter of their breathing broke in a final delicious, panting, clutching surge that lasted and lasted, and he hung within it, suspended like a sun ray.

He covered her with his body then, and from far away heard her contented chuckle, felt her nibble on his ear-lobe, felt her hand stroke his hair. He wanted to tell her he loved her, to tell her how beautiful it had been and that he loved the yellow ribbons, but he was so far re-moved into a warm red restful place in his mind, a restful den filled with the scent and the sound of Christine, that speech was impossible for him. Sleep came like a sonnet.

After sleep had rested on him awhile, his dreams began—pleasant gray sprites at first, will-o'-the-wisps that danced and laughed among themselves, twisting in patterns that grew ever so subtly more sinister. The sprites stood up and stared at him, then turned cold, turned hard and cylindrical, and surrounded him, edging closer, crowding him, pushing in around him, pressing down on his chest, smothering him. Flickering data from his brain told him this wasn't real, that it was a nightmare and would pass, but he must not scream, must not cry out, because terror screams in the night threw the cell block into panic. Subliminal strength took over, and as the gray sprites became the bars of his cell, he began to fight. He fought not the inanimate deadly bars but his own fear and loneliness, fighting his own desire to scream and struggle, his own resistance. He made himself as rigid as the bars and gripped the steel edge of his cot, forcing his mouth to stay closed, clenching his jaw as his fingers crushed into the steel like a life net, making it hurt to distract himself—squeezing the steel—squeezing the steel—

"Jesse, no! Stop it!" It was a cry of pain. Christine's voice brought him to awareness, and at the first unfocused level of thought it seemed like the steel under his fingers was frail and animate, and he let it slide from his grasp. The poignant comfort of the airy cotton bedclothes and smooth mattress murmured to him that he was at home and no longer in prison. He came partly awake, not opening his eyes, breathing deeply, trying to shake away the closed-in feeling, the lingering suffocation, the sickening uplift of nausea. His arms and legs were leaden in a trance paralysis, but then he thought, No, I must have been holding on to Chris and I've let her go, so some part of my will must function. He forced himself through the stinging agony of sleep needles to sit and put his face in his hands.

"Jesse, are you all right?" Christine snapped on the bedside light.

He felt bitter, bitter shame. Yes, he had his own weaknesses, flaws here and there in his mental fabric that he would as soon have done without, but damn it, they had never been this juvenile. Nightmares. Claustrophobia. A short attention span. They were random neuroses that he might have sympathized with if he had discovered them in another human being. In himself they aroused only self-disgust and anger. He had told himself that his months in prison were over and that he could stop reacting to them. Why this strident aftertaste?

Her hand came, a tentative pressure on his shoulder. He lifted his face from his hands, blinking against the light, and turned to her. Her eyes were sleep shadowed, her voice strained.

"Is everything okay, honey?"

"Yes. I'm sorry I woke you." He forced reassurance into the words. "A nightmare, I think. It's gone now." He lifted her hand and kissed the firm ridge of her knuckles. "I must have grabbed your arm. Did I hurt you?"

"No. But I was startled." She smiled at him lovingly, and, winking into the sudden light, he never guessed that she was acting too.

chapter five

Dance studios, by strict tradition, tend to be utilitarian, if not downright shabby. No frills. One school where Indiana took daily class in New York had been so cold that half the class was usually out with the flu. Once he had banged his skull on an exposed water pipe during one of his bravura leaps and spent the night in a hospital with a concussion.

When Christine had started her own ballet school, she didn't want stark or pristine or shabby. She wanted to teach very little girls, and stark didn't seem to suit very little girls. She had given one wall a mirror, of course, because serious students had to become accustomed to one. There was a beautiful teak barre. She had asked her first students to choose the wallpaper, and now a bright print of rainbows, stars, and clouds gave three sides of the room an appealing play-school quality. The floor

was the best, with a basket-weave undercushion to soften
the shock of each landing. It was a luxury that even
professional dancers rarely enjoyed. Most theatrical stage
floors were made for symphony, chamber music, or
drama—anything but ballet, though ballet companies
had to use them too. They were so darn hard that pro-
longed exposure left dancers with tendonitis, bone spurs,
bruising, and a complex about their beat-up feet. Indiana
had once remarked to Jesse that when you took a dancer
to bed the last thing you could coax off was her shoes.

While Indy approved of the floor in Christine's studio,
his first glance at the wallpaper had held the pained
amusement of the topflight pro looking at a dabbler.
"This is no place to turn out dancers," he had said.

And Jesse, who understood that side of Christine so
well, had shot back, "She's not trying to turn out dancers.
She's trying to turn out human beings."

It was fortunate he *did* understand, because the way
she did things, this wasn't what anyone would call a
lucrative proposition. Turning an old health food restaurant into a dancing school had taken a good chunk out
of the trust fund of hers that Jesse tried so hard not to
have any Old World male hang-ups about. She remembered the only argument in their courtship about her
money and his lack of it: the row had ended with her
emptying her wallet into her food processor and making
it eat fifty dollars while the man who was sixteen before
he owned a pair of pants without knee patches stood
gaping at her like she had just shot him in the foot. It
had seemed to do something for him, because when she
asked him with a flaming look if he was happy now, he
had whispered that she was a crazy, crazy girl and had
made love to her on the kitchen floor. With a sack of

potatoes by her head and Jesse's lips a fiery pressure on her throat, he had told her for the first time that he loved her.

The dancing school had been a tactful place to get rid of a little money—well, to be honest, a lot of money.

Her preballet class of four year olds made a straggling line in front of her. Smiling at the tiny faces, she stretched out her arms. Imitating her, they stretched out a little space around themselves. It was perfectly useless, of course. By the time she finished their warm-up, they would have bunched themselves together in a space two feet square and very likely backed her against a wall as well. How she loved them—the round tummies and sturdy legs, the plump shoulders and tumbling barrettes. Heather, in grubby pink tights and a Mickey Mouse T-shirt, was hopping up and down ecstatically for no discernible reason. Kelly was wearing a leotard of a particularly startling and iridescent lime, pulling her gum out of her mouth in a slack line that dipped heart-stoppingly close to Megan's pigtails. Robin and Melissa were trying to stomp on each other's toes, and Jamelle had deserted the line and was licking long streaks into the clean mirror with the flat of her pink tongue. As her sister in New York, who had one of the critters herself, said, you can always tell a four year old but you can't tell 'em much.

They were too young to learn ballet. In fact, classical ballet was a highly refined discipline that required a very specific musculature, and careless training on an undeveloped body was likely to produce a child with faulty skeletal alignment. However graceful ballet might appear to an audience, its unnatural positions were an ungodly strain on the body. When a teenager in her advanced class had confided that she wanted to be a doctor, not a dancer, Christine had said, "Good!" But one of her students had gone on to the corps de ballet of a prestigious Pennsylvania company, and that had put an end to Indy's remarks about plié parlors, tutu worship, and lightweight methodology.

Her own career as a dancer had been over at eighteen, when, after her adolescence had been sacrificed to daily classes, her mother had dragged her to auditions at every major ballet company in the country. Twelve companies had rejected her before the nervous breakdown (her mother's), and Christine had tucked her tail between her legs and taken her not-quite-good-enough-to-make-it body off to college like a whipped puppy. Four years at college and three spectacularly lousy attempts at romance later, just when she was becoming convinced that she was being punished for the sins of a past life, God had changed his whole attitude toward her and sent Jesse. Not that Jesse had been the man of her dreams. Oh, no. Her dreams had never been that lavish.

Warm-ups came first. It was important to start good habits early. Then she spent a moment or two teaching her imps some basic ballet terms. After that they played dance games, anything she could think of to pass on to them her joy in moving to music. Except that she never had to pass it on. It came naturally to the little pixies at this age.

Christine had started to put on a record when she noticed Kelly poking the gum strand back into her mouth, with hairs attached.

"Kelly! Do I look like a ballerina?" she asked, making a little backward *bourrée* and, at the same time, exaggerated gum-chewing motions with her jaw. She got a sardonic nursery-kid's grin from Kelly for that, and while her tiniest pupil went off to toss her gum in the waste-basket, she put on the record and asked what the music made them think of.

"It's like springtime."

"Like flying things—butterflies."

Knee-high ballerinas filled the room, leaping, balancing on one leg, arms flowing. Small fingers fluttered, small limbs waved like petals.

She joined them, going up on pointe, raising one foot in *passé*, feeling a tug in the sore thigh muscle that she had earned herself last night in her well-meant enthusiasm for wrapping Jesse up in her legs. The memory gave her a dumb grin, and flying butterflies danced inside of her as well as out. Last night's climax had left her fluttery all morning. Even now her body could recreate shadow sensations of him against her that would turn her blood into hot oil. Her eyelids began to droop. Feeling springtime and melodies inside, she began a drift dance, sweetly erotic thoughts of Jesse floating through her mind like brilliant white clouds.

Jesse, standing in the doorway, saw her flowing and lithe in her slick blue leotard and cranberry leg warmers. Her hair was falling out of its ponytail in a dusting of cherry-colored curls on her cheeks and temples. Her face, composed in reverie, was a study of innocent and powerful sensuality. Virginal. He smiled. As far as she was concerned, that was the ultimate insult. She detested her youthfully dewy prettiness. Whenever anyone told her that in twenty years she'd appreciate her *jeunesse*, she'd only roll her eyes in exasperation. When she'd dropped off their newspapers for recycling at a drive at the high school, the principal had demanded a hall pass. The first night he'd introduced her to his brothers, Sandy had given him a sparkling grin, lifted an eyebrow, and said, "She's a nice girl, Jess—but she sure does look like a minor." That, of course, had been before Sandy saw her in a leotard.

Christine's pint-sized students had begun to notice him leaning against the door frame, and they stopped dancing one by one to look knowingly at one another, and at him. They started to giggle but hid the noise behind their small square hands when he placed a finger on his lips.

Lost in the music and her pleasant thoughts, Christine heard the soft stifled laughter but assumed that someone had improvised an exuberant pratfall. Then she heard a light quick step. Warm arms encircled her waist. Warm lips softly touched her mouth. The elfin giggling grew loud and irrepressible as she opened her eyes on her husband. She pulled back, still in the circle of his arms, and when he opened his eyes also, she crossed hers and made what her sister in Boston called a caterpillar face.

"This is all very well, Mr. Ludan," she said, "but if you stay you're going to have to put on a tutu."

"Do they come in my size?"

Tingling energy from his pressureless touch on her waist was radiating all the way to her tiptoes. "That depends on what it is."

Bending closer, he breathed the answer in her ear and pulled back, grinning to watch her blush and clear her throat and make a caterpillar face again.

"That will do, Mr. Ludan." She pushed him off and he went into her office to work on her accounts for her like a good Brownie while she finished class. The crunch of gravel and purr of motors outside let him know when parents began to arrive for their little ones. When he returned to the classroom, Christine was alone, securing a record in its jacket. Lifting it from her hands, he read, "'Twinkle Toes: Beautiful Ballet Music for the Little Ballerina.' Hmm...'Lady Bug Waltz, Dancing Rain-drops, Dance of the Bee'...now I see what's been miss-ing from my day. No 'Dance of the Bee.'" He dropped a kiss on her shoulder and walked through the open door to her back room to shelve the record. "I did last month's books for you."

She put her head around the door, working the rubber band out of her pony-tail. "How'd I come out? Am I rolling in it or broke?"

"Let's put it this way—you put to death the old myths about rich girls being good with money." He dodged the rubber band she shot at him. "You know, Chris, you wouldn't do half-bad if you'd collect on some of those overdue accounts."

"Watch it, kid. I might tell your pinko friends what a closet capitalist you are." She made a bristling mustache under her uptilted nose with one burnished red curl and advanced on him, wringing her hands and cackling vil-lainously. "And now, my pretty, either pay your ballet bill or I'll repossess your hovel. Or—" Freckled fingers grabbed his lapels and jerked him full into her body. Her voice lowered a sultry octave. "Or you will submit your-self to me."

Her fingers spread flat on his chest, moved slowly downward over his cotton shirt, and got fresh with the zipper on his jeans. His body was gullible enough to heat and ache under the welcome invasion. Grinning weakly, he said, "Promise you'll be gentle."

The hand left his body, made another mustache, and twirled it before she seized him in a firm grip and dragged his lips toward hers.

"Your pleas avail you nothing!" she hissed, covering his mouth with her soft, soft lips after gently wetting their cool dry surface with her tongue. Yet she took a swift step backward out of his tightening embrace. "I think maybe I'll take your hovel instead. It might be safer. Want to go out for beer and pizza?"

"Not tonight. Tonight we picnic. I'm going to surprise you in a minute. Just wait in here."

"In here! A dank closet!"

With her glowing moistness stinging on his lips, he pulled on the light cord and shut the door on her. "In a minute."

She was a good sport and crouched by the mop and bucket listening to muffled sounds from the other side of the door, and tucked her hand on a stomach that had begun to quiver at the delightful luxury of having someone to pamper her once more. To distract herself from the sudden unwanted tears that rose under her lashes, she rapped on the door and called out, "I don't think you could have done much thinking about how this is going to look in my memoirs. Locking your wife in a closet . . ." She could hear his soft answering laughter through the door. "Anyway, you're supposed to lock Grandmother in the closet and let Red Riding Hood provide the goodies."

"Tonight," came his voice, "the wolf brings the goodies."

The studio lights were out when she emerged, but a chimneyed candle lit a pretty quilt and floor cushions that were laid with two china place settings: shrimp on crushed ice, fresh salad, chicken with paprika, and crystal wineglasses. She reclined on the pillows with a sigh, smiling at the unearthly haremlike image. Gliding down beside her, Jesse caught the direction of her glance.

His light gesture indicated their reflections in the mirrored wall. "I hope that other couple will leave us alone."

Leaning forward to brush her forefinger lovingly over his chin, she said, "I'm not worried. They'll probably be too preoccupied to glance our way. Jesse, thank you for thinking of this."

A slight movement of his head brought his lips to the tip of her finger, pushing lightly against the pad. "I like to cater to your every whimsy."

She was leaning toward him, the low bodice of the leotard outlining her breasts, exposing the gingery warmth of the skin above. The straps of the garment were fragile, curving over her straight shoulders, and he found himself half-feeling the light tug that it would take to draw the strap down over her arm. The sheer practice clothes gave her body drama. She was a fantasy image, a tiny dancer in pointe shoes, the eloquent wish fulfillment of every man who loved the sensuality of ballet and dreamed of carrying one of the lovely, ethereal creatures to a couch and slowly undressing her. She had been perspiring slightly; a few fleecy wisps around her face were still darkened from it, and it fascinated him that she could lend glamour even to sweat.

The lovely, ethereal creature put a shrimp in her mouth, made a blissful face, and was still munching when she said, "When did you get time to do all this?"

"On and off during the day. I worked at home today— I couldn't get anything done downtown. Come here, Chrissie." He pulled her toward him, turning her around, and settled her against his body between his thighs. His lips were in her hair. "I want to feed you."

The soft note in his voice had left her a little breathless, and the pressure of his hand sliding around her, coming to rest under her breasts, brought a throbbing pulse to her throat. Opening her lips to receive a bit of chicken from his fingers, she leaned back into his chest, savoring their closeness.

"Did you have a nice visit with your family last night?"

"My family . . ." he repeated absently, as though he'd forgotten who that was. "Sure. They don't change." He fed her again, and then showed her the label on the wine bottle. "Do you know what this is?"

"Yes! Because the words look like proper names in a Russian novel. Is it a Hungarian wine?"

"Uh-huh." He rested the bottle on the floor between her legs and began to perforate the cork. "It's Tokaji Aszú. Uncle Vilmos sent my father a case."

"Are you serious? You mean the wine of the kings?" Her voice became dreamily ecstatic. "The favorite vintage of Louis the Fourteenth and Frederick the Great . . . grown in the rich volcanic mountainous soil in your family's vineyards for seven centuries . . ."

His laughter produced warm exhalations that penetrated to her scalp. "Oh, we had a scraggly vine or two."

"*And* a title," she took delight in reminding him, aglow with the romanticism of his family history. She heard him mutter something about the meaninglessness of hereditary nobility, especially in families like his who hadn't had two forints to rub together since the sixteenth century, as he always did whenever she brought it up. His legs were a warm saddle around her hips. She could feel the seams of his jeans through her thin tights, and behind her, his chest and stomach were a hard cloak of warming flesh. His hand brushed her thigh as he withdrew the bottle. She shivered.

In the mirror she watched the play of his fingers as

he fed her, the way his long hand curved around the bowl of the goblet as he touched it to her lips. Their images in the mirror were light, angular, and graceful, picked out of the black mirror by the brightly burning candle flame.

Presently he murmured, "You know, don't you, child, that you're in trouble." His fingertips were lightly rubbing, touching along the soft swell of the underside of her breast. "I've put something in the sauce that makes me irresistible."

"Really?" She tipped her head to look at him. "I'll have to keep the leftovers under lock and key."

This time when she sipped, the wine was nearly gone and the backs of his fingers were tracing slowly, slowly across her lower lip. In slow motion his hand, holding the wineglass, drifted down to rest on his raised knee. She was concentrating on the hypnotic flow of his arm until, through the unguarded part of her mind, a sudden flow of image and sensation came together as she saw in the mirror his hand flat against her side, then moving up to very gently cup underneath her breast with a warm, lifting feel. His hair falling over his forehead, he bent to nuzzle in her curls and down the crescent of her throat in a movement so soft it might have been only his breath. His tongue, in passing, played over her earlobe and the outer terrace of her ear within its graceful curves. A hot liquid heaviness filled her breast where he held it, and she began to breathe in long slow deep inhalations. He smoothed over nipples that had become tight and tender against his fingers.

"Chrissie, will you tell me something?" His finger traced down her cheek. His voice was soft. "Did I hurt you last night?"

It was difficult to collect herself enough to imagine

what he meant. And then she remembered her arm this morning, with its livid print of his hand. Jesse's nightmare. The nightmare that had become hers. Her chest tightened and, close as he was, he felt her tension and said gently, "It's all right; you can tell me. Talk to me. Last night when we were making love it seemed . . . difficult for you, physically."

Her tension collapsed into a smile that measured her relief. Not the nightmare. She would not have to lie to him. She lifted her chin, straining to look upside down into his green eyes.

"You mean last night when I was—" Her hesitation stretched, becoming patently obvious.

With amused comprehension, he finished for her. "A little dry, sweetheart."

Four years of marital intimacy with an uninhibited lover had taken her beyond the point where that much frankness would produce a blush, but that didn't spare her the attendant emotions. Dry. Really. You'd think he could have found another way to put it, being a writer. But her look of reproach began to defrost under the steady stroke of his hand.

"I don't know . . ." She had to swallow. "Maybe it was hormones, or—Jess, you're making it kind of hard to speak." His husky laughter tickled the back of her neck. "Or it might have been the excitement."

"I was afraid it might have been the lack of it."

"Oh, no, I was really flying. It was nothing mental, only physical, and it got better soon. It felt a little bit like I was losing my virginity again."

"I felt a little bit like I was taking it, but none too kindly." He pulled her very close, nourishing her in his arms, and touched his lips to hers lightly, once, twice, in movements of tantalizing sweetness. Then, cradling her head in his palm, he lowered her to the floor. "I was worried that it might make you afraid the next time we made love."

"Whenever that's going to be..." The gentle thrust of his knee inside her thighs made a gush of desire fill all of her, drowning thought. Her practice leotard had an oily slipperiness that eased the path of his hands, helping her savor the size and texture of his palm as it came to rest over her breast, outlined so perfectly as she lay on the quilt beneath him. And he felt the soft, giving flesh push upward against his palm as her breathing quickened and deepened, and the firmer feel of her nipple lifting with desire. He bent to kiss it.

"It wasn't your hormones," he murmured, his tongue making unhurried circles over the liquidy fabric.

"Wh-what?"

"Ladies who go without stimulation for a while can sometimes—sometimes—God, Chrissie..." His words dissolved into a thick inhalation as her hand slipped under his belt and into his jeans.

"You were saying," she breathed, "about ladies who go without stimulation?"

"They—they—oh, my *God*." Gasping and laughing, he caught her wrists and pressed them into the quilt. "Do you want this to take a while or do you want it to be over in about twenty seconds?"

And when she widened her eyes and said, "Hell, no. I want a man with a slow hand," they collapsed together giggling idiotically and shivering, their hands coursing over each other until he pulled her on his lap and undressed her, telling her the Hungarian words for each part of her body as he kissed it, laughing at her accent when she repeated the words.

He gave her more wine, and when it spilled on his

unsteady fingers, he put them to her mouth, watching her lick them, and then dipped up a tiny crystal of melting ice and cradled her against his body while he spread the dripping bead all over her lips. She tangled her hands in his hair, moaning as his mouth descended to the cold, distended polish of hers, heating it again with his kiss.

Sliding beneath his body was a gradual movement threaded with dizzying pleasure. He lifted his mouth to hers, teasing open her lips slowly with small strokes of his own. His husky whisper came. "Open your mouth, Chris. More... I love you. I love—being with you. Don't ever let me go away again, Chrissie—stay close...close..." Her returning kisses were vibrant with love, full and deep, touching into the pain within them both, healing, searing at the crisp hurt. He felt so warm lying on top of her, his long legs stretched across her as they kissed. She let her own legs fall open so that the warmth of his hard-muscled thigh was between them, and she was rocking imperceptibly against it, losing herself in the tightening pressure. Desire seemed to be wedging itself into her, making her body feel open and empty.

"Jesse..."

His hand moved over her lower belly, lying between her open thighs where his leg had been, and the urgency she felt there spread throughout her. She reached her hands up to his back, slipping them under the light sweater, moving them slowly up. With a humorous look, he straightened away from her and held his arms over his head so she could pull it the rest of the way off. And then he folded it into a neat soft square and tucked it under her head like a pillow, looking down at her. The candlelight flickered over his skin lovingly, leaving it golden, dappled with darkness in the lean hollows and curves of his chest, his ribs. She ran her palms over his flat stomach, over his hard chest. His vitality seemed to be burning so close to the surface, like heated blood leaping to warm her hands.

"Don't stop touching me." His voice was no more than a ragged whisper, a strand of breath. "Your hands feel so good to me—so good. *Kérem,* Christine... *kérem.*"

Please, he had whispered to her, and the desperate plea stayed with her as though it were the fragrance of some sweet fading flower as they became one in the candlelight in a golden cloud of rippling movement, tawny skin and dusky hollows changing in the light like the sun's play on a brook through the leaves of a maple.

They lay together afterward with her head against his heartbeat, his hands idling over her moist, kiss-stung flesh, his lips touching her brow. Her arms and legs felt solid to her, pressing downward in deep relaxation, but inside she was quivery, a water droplet trembling on a blade of grass.

"Jess, what were you trying to tell me a while back?"

After a dreamy pause, "Hmmm?"

She pulled herself up on one elbow. "About women. When they haven't made love recently."

"Oh. That. Just that sometimes it creates a temporary problem with lubrication when they resume relations. If I had been more patient last night..."

She stopped him with a kiss. "Why is it that you always know everything about everything? Where was that from—Masters and Johnson?"

He stroked her chin with a lazy finger. "I don't remember." He gave her a sudden half smile. "More likely 'The Playboy Advisor.'"

Lovingly she stretched out her arm to caress his chest, and he turned his head to brush his mouth over the inside of her wrist. But something arrested the motion. Jesse sat up with a questioning look, taking her arm in a gentle grip.

Chris felt the warmth within her begin to chill. He was looking at the marks his fingers had left in her flesh. She watched in mute panic as he released her, pulled on his jeans, snapped on the overhead light, and then returned to sit opposite her and pick up her wrist again.

Silvery fluorescence brightened the marred fabric of her skin. The bruises were dark among the innocent freckles, broken like wine stains into discolored pools of red and purple, evoking their creation in pain and violence. For a moment he hallucinated his nightmare. Nausea cramped him. His lungs contracted in a dry spasm. What inner blindness had led him to believe that he could never harm her, even in sleep? His heart began to hammer as he studied the marks, trying to assess the force it would have taken to leave that much damage. Oh, God. He would have had to twist her arm half off. Finally he looked up into her face. Her expression was frozen, vulnerable, and she withdrew her arm from his hands and began to gather the quilt around her naked body.

"I could have broken your arm. And you only told me you were startled."

Her fingers moved nervously on the quilt, tightening it over her breasts. "I knew you'd be upset. You've already been upset enough lately. It looks much worse than it is. Hey, Jess, c'mon, it's no big deal." There was a tremor in her voice. "It was an accident."

"I could have broken your goddamn arm." The words

were close to a shout. Christine felt the fragile peace she had been living within shatter around her.

"I don't know why you're mad at me." She tried to make her voice light and to smile, but her mouth could produce only a pained twist. "I'm just the victim."

He brought her against his chest with appalling swiftness, and when he spoke, each word had a scalpel precision. "Don't ever call yourself a victim again," he whispered, the softness of the words erasing nothing from their force. "Do you understand?"

His hands left her in a sharp movement and her own failures came tumbling down on her, cold failures that pierced the final afterglow of their lovemaking, and the last warmth fled her body. The wine taste was strong in her mouth, faintly sticky and sour. And she thought, What am I going to do? Dear God, what can I do? He's losing faith in himself. And he's losing faith in me because I won't face the new dark corners in him.

He had gone to stand near the mirror, his hands clenched on the barre at his hips. Frigid-blue artificial light cut shallow patterns on his bare chest and revealed the hardness of his legs through the age-softened denims.

She wanted to get up and dress, but the brief period of nudity it would require seemed suddenly like an excruciating ordeal. The still-flickering candle flame caught her distraughtly wandering gaze. How the harsh fluorescence had dwarfed the flame. It had become an anachronism, an oddly embarrassing reminder of the past sweet moments, a stubbornly glimmering symbol oblivious of its inappropriateness.

She looked back at Jesse. Damn him. He was closing up. She could see it happening. And here she was alone with the fear. And she was so tired of being alone, and so tired of being afraid. Why was this happening to her? There must be some mistake. Problems like these belonged to the old Christine, who never quite understood how to put her life in order. She thought of Indiana's warning, that she had been bartering her inner security. Now even that had failed, and she didn't know how to help either of them anymore.

"I'd like to know what I'm being accused of." Her words were sudden, fierce, and his answer was as close to expressionless as she had ever heard from him.

"Is that what I was doing?"

"Oh. Well, weren't you, then? Then everything's okay, I guess. You weren't accusing me of anything."

Jesse held her in a gelid stare during the echoing silence that followed. Then he said, "I hate it when you playact in a fight."

It was by far the cruelest thing he had ever said to her. He knew her sensitivity; he knew she had to build walls to guard that secret inner person. Her defenses were not external armor; they were part of her chemistry, and he had never attacked them. She retreated farther into the quilt, cold fibers sharp against her cold skin. There was a moment of sheer terror as he walked over to pick up his jacket and she thought he was going to leave, just like that. But he fished in his jacket pocket for something.

"I've started smoking again, Chris. I'll probably quit, but I haven't organized the energy yet." She watched numbly as he drew a pack of cigarettes from his jacket. "If you want me to go outside, that's all right with me."

"No." Her stiff lips made the brief word more brief, a chipped syllable. She knew he'd smoked at one time, that he'd quit in college, but that had been before she knew him. It was a stranger who stood against the barre with a lit cigarette in his mouth.

"I don't know you right now," she said. "Out of nowhere I'm the enemy and I don't know what I've done wrong."

"What you've done wrong . . . who'd be able to accuse *you* of doing anything wrong? You don't do wrong things, do you, Chris? You're too damned careful. Inflexibly ladylike to the end, spoon-feeding me tolerance and compassion as if that could wipe out six months in prison. Christine, it's sticking all over me like hot tar, and I'd tear myself open to keep it from messing you up too. But what am I supposed to do if you won't tell me when that's happening?"

"Jesse, I don't want to fight. I can't stand fighting with you like this." Grasping for a compromise, watching him swallow smoke and release it in an unbroken line, she said, "You think I should have told you about the bruises. I think you should be more understanding about why I didn't say anything. Okay. We're both equally guilty. So let's drop it, okay?"

The closed expression vanished from Jesse's high-boned face. "What does equality have to do with it? What are we—Noah's animals marching off to the ark, two by two, equal this and equal that? I want to know why you've refused to respond to a single thing I've said."

"All right, *all right*." Clutching the quilt around her, she staggered awkwardly to her feet, sending an empty wineglass rolling across the floor in spinning circles. "You want a response? All right, we'll do everything your way. If you so much as breathe on me the wrong way, I'll climb all over you! I'll berate you for hours on end! No"—she was losing control completely—"I'll call the DA and ask him to begin a John Doe investigation!"

"Or," he said with false mildness, "you can go to Indy and tell him all about it."

She fell very still. In a quiet voice, she said, "How did you know I saw Indy?"

"Angela Currie mentioned seeing you with Indy strolling in Walker's Point yesterday. She honked her horn half a dozen times, but neither of you noticed."

"You don't say." She could feel herself paling. "I hope she didn't leave out the times Indiana and I were seen together necking at Packers' games." Suddenly she was on her knees weeping into the quilt, and she could hear herself say in a serrated whisper, "I only wanted someone to tell me it was going to be all right."

She knew he had come to stand near her, and she knew he was looking down at her bent shoulders even though she couldn't see his face. But he made no move to take her in his arms, which had never happened before, and she wanted to ask him to, but somehow she couldn't.

"I know," he returned softly, and came down beside her, sitting on his heels, lifting her chin. "Please don't let me harm you again. I don't know how to make you understand what it does to me."

It was much later, driving home beside him, that she realized he hadn't said it was going to be all right.

chapter six

It was not all right. The dream returned.

It began with Bach—"Air on the G String." This was one of the few classical pieces he could actually identify, because whenever Christine played it, he would ask her for the name, and when she answered he would say, "The which string?" making her repeat it until she would laugh and throw something at him and call him a philistine.

He heard Bach, and saw the cell around him, and felt Christine at his side. The bars were a moving pattern, a carousel pierced by an intermittent light like the sun through a thunderstorm. This time when the room shrank, the bars multiplied, and he could feel Christine's horror racing with his, beyond his, and he needed desperately to protect her. He wanted to reach out to the bars and drag them away from her, but some slight murmur in his brain reminded him not to touch anything, not to use his hands. It was wrong; it might hurt Christine. So he lay still as a rock and didn't scream, didn't move as the bars came closer, crushing him. . . .

When he woke, the moon was out and shining through the open window and a mist of sweat nipped his skin, making a clammy pool between his shoulder blades. He jerked his head up to look for Christine but—relief— she was lying next to him, curled like a fawn, sleeping soundly. He lay staring at the ceiling until the dawn birds began their song and an orchid-pink glow of sunlight formed on the windowsill.

The next night he didn't sleep at all, but lay watchfully quiet beside her. The clock's red digits said one forty-five when he got up, pulled on jeans and a T-shirt, and went downstairs for his jacket.

The whoosh of the heavy front door woke Christine as he went out, and then it was she who waited, blinking in the dark until he returned thirty minutes later scented of the spring night and more faintly of cigarette smoke. He slid nude into the bed, and she put her arms around him.

"Jess, can't you sleep?"

"No. It's nothing. Don't worry."

She gently rubbed his shoulder and the curve of his neck. His muscles had the pliancy of granite. She could feel his tension, his isolation. He was staring at the ceiling, not acknowledging the movements of her hands, and she wondered if he was even aware of them. The stranger. Searching for a way to bring him back, she said, "Can I get you some warm milk? A glass of wine?"

He leaned over the kissed her lips. "I've tried that."

She persisted. "Want to make love on all fours?" She

heard him choke, and, sleepily encouraged, she said, "Maybe I should slip into my diamond-and-leather garter belt and tie myself to the bed for hot sex."

He turned on his side to be closer to her, making the bedcover ruffle up against her face in a puff of air. He laughed a little and pulled it back down. His lips touched her cheek briefly. "Go back to sleep, Chris."

"Don—" Her voice went up an octave as she yawned. "Donna Crosby across the street says her husband ties her up all the time. She says I ought to get you to tie me up."

"Tell you what. Instead of giving the Crosbys a box of fudge at Christmas, we'll go over and tie them both up."

The tip of her nose twitched and she snuggled closer to him and rubbed it on his chest. "Did you ever want to tie me up, Jess?"

"With yellow ribbons, maybe . . ."

He kept her close to him and stroked her until she fell asleep, but he couldn't follow her and he watched the sun rise again.

The day was long and irritating because he couldn't seem to get the editorial bureaucracy in gear to cut through the red tape and put him quickly back on his court beat. When he came back from work, he found Christine in the rear garden in his stretched and faded Marquette sweat shirt. She was bending over a yellow plastic pail filled with scarlet parrot tulips and daffodils bright as chicks. He scooped her up with an arm under her shoulders and another under her knees, and the pail knocked against his legs to tip grassy water on his pants. He planted kisses on every part of her wind-ruddied cheek that came into range, and his face was full of her hair as he said, "My day really bit it, sweetheart. Hope you did better."

She slapped his back heartily with her free hand. "I did great! This afternoon I withdrew our savings from the bank and used the money to buy a handful of magic beans."

"In the morning we have a beanstalk to the clouds?"

"No." She grinned. "Chili. Mr. Jaroch was over, by the way. He wanted us to sign a petition demanding that the Crosbys cut their grass and take the Christmas lights off their pine. But I said the Crosbys were our friends and how their lawn looked didn't matter to us, so we wouldn't sign."

"I agree. Their grass is irrelevant. What we need here is a petition to make Crosby stop tying up his wi—" Her hand trying to cover his mouth, her scandalized laughter, and her urgent glance at the open windows next door stopped his voice. He carried her into the house, Christine struggling and trying to defend herself with the pail, leaving a trail of flowers all the way to the bedroom, where they made love half in, half out of their wet clothing.

It was afterward, while he was lazily picking grass and bits of stem from her breasts and his mouth, that he said, "Chris, I've been thinking."

"Uh-oh."

He took a little floss of her hair between his fingers and let it run through, enjoying the way it caught the spring sunlight. "I think I'd better sleep in the other bedroom for a while."

She studied him for a time in a painstaking way and finally said, "You think it might help your insomnia?"

"Yes."

"Well. All God's children gotta sleep. So be it, then."

In the kitchen an hour later she was poking at the chili in the Crock-Pot with a wooden spoon. I've got to let him do what he thinks he needs to do to feel better, she was thinking. It's not even a question of letting him—I must support him. He knows what he needs. But a tear slipped off her nose and burst into steam on the beans and she said aloud, "There's not a bit of magic in you damn things. Not a bit."

Someone—Jesse's father, she thought—had told her once that partners in marriage were like the opposite ends of a carpenter's level. What came to one came to the other. Even unspoken, their shared desperateness to mend the balance brought them closer. That was how it was supposed to work.

It was not easy for her to chart the undercurrents because none of them were familiar. The only easy thing would have been to let her imagination run wild as she lay alone in her bed speculating about the things that made it difficult for Jesse to fall asleep beside her. On every rational plane, she knew that none of this came about through some failing of hers, though below the surface, doubts stirred that never resolved themselves into thought. She told herself that she was too strong to become involved in a meaningless welter of self-reproach. She was too mature not to cope with the first true crisis in their lives together.

Yet vividly real, indelible, was the image of David Harris going to federal prison for refusing to serve in the Vietnam War and leaving his wife Joan Baez. They had been dedicated, they had been strong, they had been in love, but when David Harris came home from serving his ideals, neither his will nor hers had been enough to save their marriage.

Probably that had nothing to do with what would
happen between her and Jesse. She wished she could
stop thinking about it. At times she was afraid her thwarted
emotions would spill down around her in a landslide. A
week passed without that, however, and though there
were probably things she and Jesse weren't telling each
other, and they did not make love, and Jesse continued
to be uncharacteristically tense and distracted, there were
moments of fun, and there was companionship. Life had
a strange way of tricking you into being much braver
than you really were, as she had discovered while Jesse
was in jail. Mundane tasks intruded into every tragedy;
the necessary rituals of eating, sleeping, and clothing the
body had to be followed, giving structure to the suffering.

Jesse played soccer on Thursday evening.

Beyond the hilltop field of ragged municipal grass, a
light lake wind tickled the pointing skyline of church
spires, steep roofs, and tall trees coming into leaf. It
sucked Jesse's soccer clothes into a hard outline of his
chest and thighs as he ran backward, watching the ball.
As the ball got closer to the wrong goal, Christine's view
was suddenly blocked by her sister-in-law Beth, one step
down from her on the bleachers, who stood up to shout,
"Get it out of there! Get it out of—" Beth collapsed with
a moan as the other team scored, one hand clutching the
bulge of her pregnant abdomen.

"Beth, are you all right?" Christine bent forward.

"No! Now we'll go into the half two points down,
because the ref is going to blow the whistle as soon as
they set up and—there, what did I tell you?"

Christine suppressed a grin as the team began to collect in front of the bleachers by the big water thermos. Even with the recent upsurge in the popularity of American soccer, the long-established ethnic teams ruled the Milwaukee leagues. The Hungarian team that Jessee and his brothers played on had been around for twenty-five years. Club Magyar. Ten years ago, if someone had told her that in another decade she would be a member of a social organization called Club Magyar, she would have said, "Huh?" Ten years ago she wouldn't have known that a Magyar and a Hungarian were the same.

Nowhere else in mid-America could you hear more people speaking in heavy accents than at a Milwaukee soccer game. In her first season Christine had heard all the languages of Babel: Latvian, Serbian, Persian, French, German, Italian, Arabic, Hungarian. According to Jesse, it was often pretty hot stuff. He said that by now she could probably go to any corner of the globe and be ready with a local oath either threatening blood vengeance or requiring it.

Jesse came toward the bleachers talking to his older brother, with Sandor's narrow arm draping his shoulders like a garland. Sandy was a taller, more prominently boned version of Jesse, and, because her brother-in-law had been growing his hair since he'd returned from combat in Vietnam, he gave Christine a fair idea of how Jesse would look in a ponytail.

Sandy looked up at his wife Beth and his face dissolved in a landscape of creases that revealed exactly what a handsome older man he would be in forty years. He jumped up on the seat beside her, tugged gently at the hem of her red sweatshirt, and said, "Hey, Jess! Want to see where I keep my extra soccer ball?" He laughed as Beth slapped his hand away. Straightening his goalie shirt, he said, "I suppose if I let another goal through I don't get dinner?"

"For a week!" Beth said, but she was grinning. "Keep playing like this, and next time we play husbands against wives, we'll murder you."

Feeling great since Jesse had come up beside her and put his hand on her knee, Christine leaned forward and feigned a shudder of revulsion. "I'll never be on another wives' team against these brutes. Last time they wiped up the field with us, twenty to one!"

Beth was unknotting the leather ribbon from Sandor's wild ponytail. "As if we'd let you quit. You made our only goal."

With a gleam of unholy amusement, Sandor said, "Jesse let that through."

"No way. It came at me like greased lightning. Even you couldn't have stopped that goal." Jesse leaned over to absorb the tantalizing vibrations of Christine's mouth. "And besides, I'm not very good with my hands."

Beth glanced up from retying her husband's neatened tresses. "That's not what the girls used to say at Pulaski High."

Watching the lightning-fast movements of Jesse's legs as he ran back to the field beside Sandor, Christine dropped onto the bench beside Beth and said amiably, "Okay, Mrs. Ludan the elder, what about the girls at Pulaski High?"

Beth provided her with enough teasing material against Jesse to last a good six months if judiciously employed. Indy arrived midway through the half. His contract with the Milwaukee Ballet disallowed everything—soccer, motorcycling, downhill skiing—that might injure the fabulous body in which the company had invested so many dollars. He said that, the way fate worked, this practically insured that he would break his neck falling off a bleacher seat.

When Christine found her way up to the top row and handed him a cold bottle of beer, he tossed his beret on her curls and arranged it becomingly.

"Where've you been?" she asked.

"I had a union meeting. What's the score?"

"We're down, four–three. It's been fierce. See the guy on the Croatians' with the black mustache? The ref just gave him a yellow card for this." She imitated the referee's motions.

"Unnecessary roughness."

"That's what I thought. He gave Sandor a nosebleed."

"Oh, Lord. Yeah. I can see it on the front of his shirt. What did Beth say?"

"A truck driver would have blushed. Jess and Peter didn't look very pleased either."

"I can imagine."

Christine caught the warm wool scent from his sweater as he took a long drink from the bottle. Then he said, "How's Jesse?"

"I don't know." Her hands clasped in her lap. "Angela Currie told him that she saw us together."

He had been settling the beer between his feet, but he turned his face toward her at that, the heavy-lidded green eyes regarding her alertly.

"It hurt him," she said. "Neither one of us has ever taken a problem outside before. What could it do but draw two red lines under how poorly we're communicating? I don't think he wanted to let it hurt, but it did."

He handed her the beer. "Drink." After she did, he

said, "Have you stopped giving up what you need?"

"I . . ." She paused. "I'm not sure."

He nodded. "Keep on it. I know I sound like a one-trick pony, Chris, but you can't put *him* back together. Only yourself." Leaning back slightly, as though to see her better, he said, "Did I ever tell you that you're beautiful?"

White shock. "No."

"You are. Your features are pretty ordinary, but—I don't know—something kind of shines from inside."

"I think I just felt a rush of nutrition to my ego."

"Good. Taking care of you right now is the closest I can come to taking care of Jesse."

"I know." She saw his pliant smile appear briefly before a roar from the spectators around them drew their attention back to the game.

Watching his brother through narrowed eyes, Indy reached blindly for the beer in Christine's hands. "He didn't need to lose that ten pounds in prison. He's out of shape."

"Yes. And it really bothers him too. Look at his face. It's inhuman that that jail doesn't have a place to exercise. He went from a tiny stuffy room with cots at night to a tiny stuffy room with tables and chairs during the day. It's inhuman."

Indy shrugged. "Economics. Who's going to get into office these days running on a platform of budget expansion for the prison system?"

The bleachers shuddered as the spectators erupted to their feet. Jesse had stopped a lightning pass from his brother Peter and broken loose from the defender at his side. In one fast, sensuous burst of power, effortless in appearance, looking like the Jesse of last summer, he

put the ball neatly through the Croatian goalie's out-
stretched arms and it bounced against the back net in a
swirl of black and white. Goal.

But even as a crowd of friends and relatives who hated
to lose were beginning to cheer themselves hoarse, the
referee blew his whistle, signaling an offside call that
meant the goal didn't count. Christine pulled the beret
down over her eyes, stuck out her tongue, and said,
"Blah."

All around them, heavily accented voices were scaling
upward in volume, and Indiana was shouting angrily,
"Offside, my ass! He wasn't offside!"

As for her husband, her fascinating, pleasant-tem-
pered, uncommonly intelligent husband, Jesse had his
well-structured nose two inches from the referee's, and
there was no mistaking the substance of their interchange.
The referee flipped a yellow card from his back pocket
and held it over his head—it was a warning. Jesse replied
with a hand signal that needed no translation. Without
wasting another second, the referee flashed up a red card,
putting Jesse out of the game. As Jess came stalking to
the sidelines, the crowd gave him an ovation, probably
because they were enchanted by this sudden, unexpected
feistiness in their favorite striker. But Christine, gripping
hard on her knees, could feel the repeated movement of
her lips as she whispered, "That's not Jesse."

"Hey, tiger, what'd you say to him?" asked someone
from the bench four rows down.

"I told him to stuff it," Jesse snapped, catching the
thrown towel, wiping his face and neck with it. He looked
angrily into the crowd and yelled, "Chris!"

It made her angry to be summoned like that, like he
was calling the dog, but he was marching off down the

sidelines with his jaw set, pulling on his sweat jacket, and his mood told her there was no depending on his coming to his senses and returning to apologize if she sat tight. You never knew, he might take off without her, and she'd have to catch a ride home with one of his brothers, which would be even more embarrassing. Darn him anyway. She hopped down and ran to catch up to his long strides.

She cleared her throat. "Evidently you don't think we should stay to the end."

"Screw it," he said succinctly. "We're going home."

Oh, we are, are we? she thought irritably. At the car he wrenched open the door for her, and then his own, more violently. She had hardly pulled on her seat belt before he ground the Chevy into gear and spun out of the parking lot with an acceleration that was a nice mate to his temper. When they stopped at the light at the end of the block, he pulled the left-turn signal. It came off in his hand with a neat snap. Christine gave a sputter of mirth; she wasn't sure why. Maybe it was the way he sat there staring with disbelief at the hapless auto part in his palm. With a heavy sigh he tossed it over his shoulder into the backseat and began to snicker too. Then they were clinging to each other's shoulders, howling with laughter, until the chest pains made them gasp and the line of cars waiting behind them became a devil's chorus of blaring horns. But in their laughter was a new note that they both heard; and that was despair.

Sandor, Peter, and a couple of Jesse's friends from the team came by after the game to see how Jesse was doing after his virgin expulsion, and they invited him to come out with them to a tavern for a "red card" party.

Jesse looked questioningly at Christine, but he seemed pleased by the sympathetic intrusion. She had the feeling that, if he stayed home, they would have a rip-roaring fight, so she gave in gracefully.

"You go right ahead, Jess. I'll spend a quiet evening at home darning your socks," she said with a mock wistfulness that masked the real wistfulness she felt.

"You're a lucky man, Jess," Sandor said, taking her into his arms and warming her all over with his lean body. "My socks are full of holes and Beth just says she likes the way my toes look poking out when I lie on the couch watching TV."

They laughed and carried Jesse off, and she wandered upstairs and, interestingly enough, actually looked in Jesse's drawer and threw out a holey sock or two, wondering how many women left in the world still darned. She could imagine her female Irish ancestors knitting their men socks by candlelight, darning them by candlelight. It was comforting to realize that Beth, very content in her traditional woman's role, didn't darn socks either.

Then Christine called her sister in Boston and ran up the long-distance bill talking cheerful nothings for half an hour. She spent from then until three o'clock in the morning making herself feel worse by drinking coffee and reading a long bleak family saga and waiting for Jesse to come home. It was beginning to show gray through the window when a taxi pulled up outside and she was awakened from a half doze by the bravura strains of something culled from the Budapest Opera repertory being sung in loud disharmony by four unruly men in the street outside, one of whom was her husband. She dragged herself to the window and watched them. They were leaning on one another, holding one another up, and trying to help Jesse find his house key, a task evidently difficult to accomplish given the state of the searchers. She descended the stairs stiffly and let him in, throwing a quick wave to the other three roisterers, who piled back into the taxi, throwing her unsteady kisses and compliments that she was glad the neighbors wouldn't be able to translate.

She got him to the couch and began to pull off his clothes, an activity that was complicated by his amorous attentions, which, though misguided, had enough instinctive expertise to be extremely arousing.

"If you can make love in this condition, Ludan, you're a medical marvel," she whispered.

He was not, however, a medical marvel. He fell asleep. But when she crawled out from under his dead weight, the motion roused him enough to gaze up at her with his splendid light eyes and say, "I love you, babe. I love you so damned much."

How nice. She covered him with a comforter, but she would as soon have smothered him with it.

Given the coffee in her system, getting up four hours later was not the undertaking it might have been.

The house was quiet as she sat at the pine table in her small country-style kitchen. She had tuned the stereo to an easy-listening station and left it on low. A long soft sigh came from her as she dropped two pieces of bread into the toaster. Why had she let it become so difficult for her and Jesse to be open with each other? She became tied up in knots inside whenever she tried to talk about him in prison, and she wondered whether it was better to be silent or to risk being insensitive. Soft-focusing on the toaster, she enjoyed the oblique fun-house-mirror effect of its aluminum side until twin swirls of smoke rose from the slots in increasingly giddy clouds.

"Damn!" she said. She'd forgotten. Three months ago, bringing in a bag of groceries by herself, carrying the keys between her teeth, she'd knocked the toaster off the kitchen cart and sent it banging to the floor. The next day it had sent up smoke signals, which was why she hadn't used it since then. The frustration of that day returned as she quickly unplugged the offending appliance and fished the two flat shards of carbon from the slots.

Waving her hand to circulate the smoke, she tried to scrape the toast and ended up with a sink of black dust and two needle-thin pieces of toast.

"So irritating!" she ground out, and stood by the sink staring at the scraps of toast she had left. She'd seen bigger postage stamps, she thought glumly, her mind drifting back to Jesse. He had gone off like a powder keg yesterday. There could be no more pretending. She couldn't continue to say "That's not Jesse" whenever he did something unfamiliar, because it *was* Jesse. It was Jesse as he had become.

She jammed the remains of the toast down the garbage disposal with a fork and turned the switch. Nothing happened. This she was used to—the disposal had a quirk. You had to flip twice. She flipped again and it worked, as it always did. But this time it had a new trick, which it played after the toast was only half-ingested: it gave a horrible grinding noise and a loud belch, and after a few seconds of disgusting suction noises, the other sink began to fill with dirty water from its drain.

She moaned and grabbed the disposal switch to turn it off. She was thinking, Have I changed too? Adversity was supposed to strengthen people. She tried to search out the new strength inside. She tried to find the something beautiful Indiana said she had. But inside she was hollow.

The base of her spine prickled and her neck was tightening as though there were a noose around it, familiar feelings when she was overwhelmed with worry. Distractions, she needed distractions. Not the saga. No more coffee. Thank goodness for the laundry. She left the cloudy kitchen and trudged up the stairs, trudging down a few minutes later with a laundry basket, leaving a small track of dirty clothes behind her down the basement steps.

A moat of dark water ringed the washing machine and she walked through it on tiptoes, shuddering as the cold sliminess touched her skin. "Yuck! Yecchhh!" she complained as she fed the clothes into the spinner. Spring rains had turned the old basement into a swamp. She should have remembered to start the dehumidifier and check the sump pump. Turning on the washing machine, morosely watching the rapid drip of water from the hose at the faucet end, she decided that it was very interesting to learn that, when one's life fell apart, everything went at once. She thought of her happy, orderly life dripping away like the leaky hose.

The washer began to spin. A new wrinkle in the warped linoleum had put the machine off perch, and it began to rock in an unholy clamor, like a bucket of bolts possessed by an evil spirit. To top it off, a weird, high-pitched scream came from the hallway above her head, and she stared up in appalled wonderment until she realized that the cloud of smoke from the burned toast had finally reached the smoke alarm in the entranceway. She plunged headlong up the steps, racing to open the kitchen door and clear the air.

But Jesse had opened the door. He was standing in

the middle of the kitchen in his bathrobe, his hair tousled, looking sleepy eyed and amiably cross. The smoke alarm stopped its nerve-tingling keening as the cloud dissipated into the backyard.

"Morning, darlin'," he mumbled, and yawned. "What's that ungodly racket in the basement? It sounds like the washing machine that ate Cleveland."

Christine had the pronounced feeling that she was on the verge of making the kind of immature scene she most despised.

Jesse seemed to come to the bleary conclusion that for a man who had come home at dawn, he was not being very diplomatic. He tried to turn it into a joke. "Christine, how many times do I have to tell you not to clean the lawn mower in the washing machine?"

"Everything's broken around here! The car and the sink and the toaster and the washer."

The words, delivered somewhere in the decibel range of an SST on takeoff, had a powerful effect on Jesse's hung-over brain. One hand opened the cupboard over the sink and groped shakily for the aspirin while he took in the lavender shadows that fringed her eyes, the smears of black soot on her cheeks, her belligerent barefoot stance.

His hand closed gratefully around the aspirin bottle. Attempting to rise to the occasion somehow, he said, "Smoke detector's working," and smiled at her. She looked murderous. He took two aspirin.

Then he caught her around the waist and brought her back with him to the plush easy chair, drawing her down against his chest, covering them both with the comforter. Tenderly he wiped the flushed, defiant face of the woman who was everything in the world to him, picking up a stray tear or two. He thought, This is the second time in a week I've made her cry. I've got to pull myself together before I hurt her any more.

Resting his cheek against her hair, he listened to her fretful choking complaints about his behavior, his appliances, his soccer game. . . . At least she'd gotten over her reluctance to fight with him.

She was gulping out, "All you do is drink with your brothers and stay out all night and never fix a thing. You don't fix a thing."

They both knew what she was really begging him to fix. Christine, I'm trying.

"I know two late nights out without you in less than two weeks was pushing things," he said. "But being with my brothers seems to help."

"Everyone helps but me."

"No. No—you help most. Most by far. Do you think you could go back to sleep if I held you?"

She sniffed.

Interpreting that as a yes, he snuggled her more comfortably against him and whispered, "When you wake up, will you let me make love to you?"

She sniffed again. And so he did.

chapter seven

Jesse's parents had resided in the South Side neighborhood of Pigsville since their arrival in Milwaukee in 1957. "Yeah," Jesse loved to tell people, "I'm from Pigsville." It was a unique area, isolated like the land time forgot in a dwarf valley that only the initiated knew how to find by threading through the potholed lanes of industrial Milwaukee, past a truck dealership, and then plunging down, down a spiraling blacktop road flanked by high airy grasses and buttercups.

An old railroad yard bounded Pigsville to the north, the forbidden playground where Jesse and his brothers had spent their Saturdays inventing elaborate games inside the decrepit sidelined boxcars and observing the constant shuffling of full ones. Just beyond the rail yard, a brewery rose like a massive red-brick cliff, puffing its roast-corn aroma of malt deliciously into the little valley.

And not thirty feet from the back bedroom Jesse had
shared with nine brothers, a colossal concrete pillar shot
upward to support the high slab of an interstate freeway,
as sturdy and awe producing as one of Goliath's legs.
Welcome to Pigsville and Pigsville Is Best, announced
ancient spray-painted messages on the pillar, greeting
Jesse and Christine as they pulled up to join the herd of
cars in front of his parents' house on Sunday morning.

The freeway would block in shade toward noon, but
it was still early enough for creamy sunlight; and it was
quiet enough to hear the robins sing because the cement
pillars seemed to capture and drown the city sounds from
the sharp bluffs above. Only the Ludans' tar-papered
bungalow showed signs of activity. The little cottages
and raised-basement houses slumbered on. A tabby cat
meowed its way through the chicory patch underneath a
rowboat up on cinder blocks in a neighbor's yard. Plan-
tain and pineapple weeds grew lushly in the little plots,
and here and there lay an inexplicable dirt heap. Spring
plantings of geraniums and petunias were already beginning to brighten everyone's window boxes. Good-
naturedly inadequate, robustly unpretentious, Pigsville
had a way of seeming to delight in its own lack of gloss.

Pigsville. Jesse, one of the few people to have re-
searched the subject, had found that the area was named
Pigsville either because of a Mr. George Pigg, who was
rumored to have lived in the valley a hundred years ago,
or because the valley was the site of a farm that had once
raised that useful animal.

As Christine was unloading a picnic basket from the
backseat and Jesse was pulling a cooler of beer from the
trunk, a series of yelled numbers exploded from behind
the bungalow, and a six-foot-tall red-and-yellow package

of french fries came running around the side of the house
into the front yard. In this ingenious costume were housed
four of Jesse's brothers and one sister, ages twelve to
sixteen, wearing nodding french fry hats and doing their
best to run in synchronization. They were doing pretty
well until one of the front french fries saw Jesse and
stopped in its tracks to shout "Hi!" The others smacked
full into it and the cardboard packaging uptilted, spilling
fries every which way on the grass in a wobbling heap
that upset the small shrine of Mary by the front porch.

They were more healthy looking than they were beautiful, these youngest Ludans—all long arms and legs and
jutting joints, torrents of light dancing hair, flecked hazel
and green eyes. All at once they picked themselves up,
reproaching one another with husky chuckles and waving
at Jesse.

Andy, who was the eldest, straightened his french fry
cap, which had come askew, and rescued the little ce-
ramic Madonna from where she'd fallen facedown in a
patch of chickweed.

"What d'you think, Jess?" He gestured toward the
voluminous costume that lay on its side like a beached
ark. "We're wearing it in the Memorial Day Charity
Marathon. Peter helped us silk screen the package."

They were remarkable distance runners, and the cos-
tumes did wonders for swelling their list of sponsors
when they ran in charity fund raisers. In the Frigid Five,
the grueling midwinter race, they had gone as a can of
worms—which their father, Janos, called singularly ap-
propriate—and had gotten their picture on the front page
of the morning paper beside a headline about national
economic ills.

They surrounded Christine and Jesse, a gaggle of grins

and T-shirts talking excitedly. Andy had grown taller
than Christine in the relatively short period of her marriage, and he emphasized it by putting his elbows on her
shoulders and giving her a greeting kiss on the top of
her head. Stepping back, he pulled down the yoke of his
T-shirt to show her his neck.

"I've got a hickey, see?"

Boy, did he ever. Christine examined it with interest.
"It's very nice. I've often wondered how people did those
things."

He gave her an amused look. "Far be it from me to
shatter your innocence if lover boy over there hasn't
taught you." Relieving her of the picnic basket, Andy
took her neck in a comfortable stranglehold and began
to walk with her toward the front porch. He was a toucher,
like the rest of his family, and Christine had been married
two years before she had stopped being afraid of and
begun envying their easy and frequent body contact.

"Weren't you just hoping it would storm today so we
wouldn't have to spend the day up north grubbing around
in the forest for mushrooms like a bunch of immigrants?"
he said.

"Have you no respect for the traditions of the old
country?" demanded fourteen-year-old Anna in a bogus
Hungarian accent that belonged unmistakably to her
grandmother. "Every year when I was a little girl Papa
would take us to Stuhlweissenburg and we would have
cold game and truffles under a white awning."

Nicholas, who was twelve, said, "You can bet she
never picked them herself. Bet they made some poor serf
do it."

"That's probably why they all went Communist and
turned the land into a state-owned farm," Anna said.

"The Ludan spring tradition—blistered feet, poison ivy, horsefly bites..."

"Stickers on your butt," Nicky finished.

His older brothers and sister pounced quickly on that lapse of tongue. "What a mouth that kid's got on him," Andy moaned. "And in front of a girl who's never had a hickey..."

Unabashed, Nicky put his wisp-thin five-foot length on Jesse's back and said, "Can I ride with you guys out to the country, please? Sandy's taking Beth on the Harley and Indy's only got room for one in the RX-7 and Andy's already claimed it. I don't want to ride with Grandma."

"What's wrong with riding with Grandma?" Jesse hitched Nicky's bottom more securely upward.

"She'll make me say a Rosary with her. She says I'm the last chance to get one of us into the priesthood, and she won't listen when I tell her I've got no vocation. And I ought to know by now, after getting up at daybreak for six months to be an altar boy for early Mass. You know what, Jess? When I grow up I'm going to be just like you and marry a Protestant and never go to church again!"

That drew whoops from his family. Under Jesse's laughing gaze, Christine tried in a flustered way to contradict Nicky's understanding of Protestant churchgoing and explain her own conduct as they walked across the porch, which creaked under their weight.

The living room was filled twice beyond capacity with Ludan relatives, children of relatives, and girl friends and boyfriends of relatives. Dodging affectionate slaps and exchanging warm embraces, she made her way with Jesse to the kitchen, where Jesse's parents were holding court around the gray Formica table. There was a coffee cup on every flat surface, and a denim-and-tennis-shoe-clad leg dangled from the scarred arm of every chair. The air was filled with talk of sports, politics, religion, weather, children, and more sports. The worn furniture was draped in jackets and sweaters. Boots, picnic baskets and coolers, baseball bats, Frisbees, and soccer balls made the floor treacherous.

The kitchen hummed with last-minute preparations of everything that was needed to feed the army of people. Grandma Ludan stood in the middle of the fray, ironing. Beth was supervising half a dozen people who were packing food. Several infants toddled blithely underfoot. Christine watched Indy scoop up Sandor's daughter, Krystal, as she padded by sucking on a teething biscuit. He peered doubtfully into the back of her pants and then felt cautiously around with his finger.

"Beth, your kid's soaked."

Beth was trying to wrap a cake without destroying the frosting. She gave Indiana a harassed look. "There's a diaper in the blue bag by Papa."

Jesse's brother Peter was near enough to the blue bag to lean sideways and fish out a diaper and because there was no room to move, he tossed it to Indiana. The high-brow aesthete and bachelor ballet superstar sat on the counter with his little niece on his lap and changed her diaper with long-practiced expertise.

Jesse's father had been tickling a baby in a sunbonnet with his broad white mustache, but he surrendered her to one of Jesse's aunts when he saw Jesse and Christine. He threw open his arms, offering an embrace. He appeared frail beside his strong, well-made children, his face marked by the years of suffering from the little-understood disease that had attacked and weakened his spine. But the orthopedic harness around his neck was bright with gold paper stars, Pac-Man emblems, and a sticker of a big green pickle with rolling eyes—all gifts from his adoring grandchildren. Grandpa's neck, he called it, and Christine had become so accustomed to it that there were times when she forgot that he couldn't hold his head upright without it.

Christine watched him take Jesse's chin in his hand and turn his son's head this way and that. "You look better, Jesse," he said in his soft Hungarian accent. "There's more color in your face."

Jesse helped his father sit back down and hitched himself on the table, with his father's gnarled brown hand on his knee. Patting his own cheek, Jesse said, "It's the prison pallor, Papa."

His father nodded, his hazel eyes full of understanding. "It will be better for you. Trust. Three years I was in the Communist labor camps when Sanyi was a baby. It never leaves you, but you get over it. I promise you. Why, look what came of it." Jesse's father extended his arms, indicating his large family.

"We know what came of it," Sandor said, holding a picnic basket. "Mama didn't have a kid for four years."

Jesse's mother, Mari, put down the celery she was slicing to pinch her eldest son's nose. "So something good comes from everything."

Christine walked quietly beside Jesse in the cathedral hush of the forest, her hands in her pockets, Jesse's in his. Filtered sunlight broke in dusty streaks through the pale-green crowns of red oak and hickory, making shifting patterns of light and shadow on the fawn-colored carpet of nutritious decay beneath. Soft ferns brushed their ankles. Mayapple and white trillium bloomed in delicate corners. Jack-in-the-pulpits stood upright in the gentle air. She listened to the hum of the bees and breathed in the cool silk scent of freshly thawed earth.

What had begun as a crowd, walking up the sloping sand lane into the forest shade, had thinned as small groups split off to hunt in their own way and under their own theories for the elusive morel mushrooms, the wilderness delicacy. There was a certain friendly rivalry about it because morels were so hard to find and so prized. Some years she and Jess had hunted them with humorous and notoriously unsuccessful zeal. In others they had wandered hand in hand on the fragrant paths, listening for the mewl of baby squirrels in their sheltered nests, viewing the dew-jeweled tidiness of a spiderweb, kissing against wide tree trunks. But today Jesse stood apart.

He could feel himself sliding back into the sedative numbness that his family had temporarily interrupted. Their boisterous exuberance had irritated him, jangling the grayness of his mood. Grayness was a good word. He could see his moods in colors now: deep purple, almost black anger; the flaxen sweetness of his intimacy with Christine; gray depression. Looking backward, he had begun to be surprised that in prison he had learned to accept the grayness as positive, a dulling of the painful processes of his environment. Now that he no longer needed it, it clung to him anyway with a whiplash tenacity. Funny, no matter how much sensitivity you thought you had to what someone might feel in a situation, you never really understood it until you experienced it yourself.

Jesse suddenly became aware that Christine was not

beside him. He turned and saw her standing off the path beside the ragged upthrust rootwork of a fallen elm, her eyes closed, her hands forward, holding a Y-shaped stick out horizontally by its top ends. Clowning again, he thought lovingly.

"What are you doing?"

"Witching!" she said, walking blindly. "You know how people witch for underground water with willow branches? Maybe it works for morel mushrooms too."

He watched her, enjoying her outdoor prettiness, the way her body moved under the pink sweater and unzipped pink and gray down vest. Coral button earrings accented her earlobes with dainty sensuality. From the back pocket of her light corduroy jeans, four pussy willow branches she'd picked earlier protruded gaily, waving like kittens' tails. But the toe of her sand-colored suede walking shoe became suddenly entangled with a straggling root and she fell on her stomach onto the soft spongy ground. "Ooof!" she said, and played possum.

He knew she was all right. With a little warning, dancers could land like a pound of loose feathers. He hesitated briefly and then flopped down beside her full length and rested his chin on his hands. After a moment she looked up at him, blinking.

"Find anything?" he asked, lifting the furry softness of a plump pussy willow catkin from her hair. The sun warmed their backs, but the air was pleasantly cool, tipping her nose and cheeks in cameo-pink. Her lips were slightly parted and wind stroked from the long slow climb up the hill, and her chest was moving softly from the exertion, her breasts touching the ground. She copied his position, putting her chin into her hands in exactly the same way he did, and when she moved that way her breasts lifted so that he could see their small perfect outline through her sweater.

"There are things I'd much rather look for," she said suddenly, her mouth shaping itself into a sultry little grin.

"Pinecones?" he suggested, drawing her vest gently back to reveal more of her body. "Another witching stick?"

"No."

"Eye of newt? Tongue of bat?"

She leaned so close to him that he could feel her breath bathe his lips.

"Tongue of Jesse," she whispered, and leaned closer, closer, until she was almost touching him, and he felt the burning caress of his desire rising within, knowing the taste of her, needing to feel it again.

Then she changed her mind, frisking away like a whisper of fox fire.

"No, no," she said, "what I'm really interested in is mushrooms." She rolled off on the amber leaves, her back turned. After a half second she looked over her shoulder at him, and her eyebrow lifted in a teasing, expectant curve that matched the sexy quirk on the corner of her lips.

The grayness inside him seemed to thaw in a sharply intensive rush of colors and he reached for her, barely touching the delicious curve of her waist before she twisted away again and grabbed a handful of leaves from the forest floor to toss at him.

"Cut it out!" She laughed. "You're trying to invade my personal space."

This time when he reached for her, adrenaline and overwhelming need made him quick and agile enough to catch her by the ankle. He pulled her beneath him, letting the soft movements of her wriggling body spire through his senses, twisting and altering the path of his swiftly warming blood.

With his eyes closed, and his mouth hovering over a lovely cheekful of freckles, he murmured, "There's one personal space of yours that I'd give heaven and earth to be able to invade right now."

"Really, Sir Toby!" she exclaimed in an enchantingly prim tone. "How can I continue as your governess if you persist in using me so disgracefully?" Taking in a staccato breath as his knee worked its way between her thighs, she added, "That does it, sir! I'm reporting this to the duchess!"

His mouth moved softly over the cool surface of her cheek. "Christine. Kiss me."

She almost let him reach her mouth before she turned her head away, smiling wickedly, biting her lower lip. "That wasn't your line. You were supposed to say, 'You're going to want this as much as I do, baby.'"

"Was that my line?" He nuzzled coaxingly into her hair, running his tongue lightly along the edge of her earlobe. "I assumed it was impossible." Pressing a body that was beginning to ache voluptuously into her, remembering the empty months without her, his voice came with petal softness against her skin. "I assume no one in the world has ever wanted this as much as I do at this moment."

"Assume nothing when dealing with members of the mysterious sex."

His light, exquisite kisses ravished the edge of her jaw and flickered over her throat. "Mysterious," he breathed. "Soft inside, warm. . . . Turn your face back to me, Christine."

Here she was, finding herself doing that despicable thing she had promised herself she would never do—using his desire for her as a weapon. But it was in a good cause. In a playful movement she lifted her face, kissed him quickly, and turned away again. "Was that enough?"

His fingers slid softly under her cheek where it pressed the ground and began to stroke her there, trying gently to make her turn toward him. "Kiss me, love," he whispered.

That note in his voice was very difficult for her to resist. And yet. . . . She looked up into the tender green eyes above her. "First will you tell me something?"

His hand formed itself to the side of her face, his thumb trembling over her lips. "Yes. What is it?"

"I only want to know—how do you feel today?"

His heart clenched at her words because she was having to learn how to beg him to open his thoughts for her. The backwash of trying to spare her his dark emotions and memories was that his silence had also become its own burden. He was beginning to realize how frozen he must have been to understand all of this so slowly, and he wondered how he would be able to share it without overwhelming her in it. All there was left in the world to need was she. And to heal.

"I feel glad to be with you," he said.

She smiled up at him, and before she closed her eyes he felt the love he saw there penetrate his deepest pain. Her lips parted and she waited for his kiss, floss-soft at first, then heady and powerful, with their bodies moving together in heavy strokes, their hands sliding into each other's hair to hold the kiss, and hold it. . . .

A gust of wind scented of moss and sunlight parted

the misty leaves far overhead, and with a papery crackle blew over the empty mushroom sacks. The sound startled her in the open, peaceful setting and she looked up, the heavy sunlight streaming into her eyes. She saw the paper bags where they had curled on their sides beside the elm, and then, as though magic had summoned them forth in some uncanny way from the fertile pile of leafage, she saw the spongy cones of many, many morel mushrooms scattered like an elfin village on the humid ground. A soft, surprised laugh burst from her.

"Jesse! Our morels!"

More interested in losing himself in her than in analyzing what seemed like some sudden obscure scruple, he said, in a vague effort to reassure her, "Don't worry about morals, Chrissie. We're married."

She had to roll him over, straddling him, and retrieve his hand from under her sweater to drop a mushroom into his palm before he cooled down enough to understand.

Their harvest filled four old-fashioned milk cans. It was the talk of the camp fire that night, breaking all family records for a mushroom mother lode. In Jesse's family, where one had barely to draw breath to get loving approval, Christine found herself all but carried around the clearing on their shoulders. Her heavily edited version of "How I Found the Mushrooms" had an attentive audience that Homer would have envied.

Her parents arrived as the thickets darkened with purple dusk and the spring peepers began to call from secret lagoons. The Ludans scrupulously invited them to all family gatherings, and her parents scrupulously attended.

From the shelter of Jesse's arm, she watched her father dock the silver Mercedes by a stand of sumac. He climbed out of the driver's seat, a small freckled man in a Pierre Cardin leather jacket—Dr. Bell. She had never known he loved her until the day they had put Jesse in prison and he had said, "I'm here if you need me, Christine," and she had found that she did.

Her mother, Sylvia, had never overdressed for an occasion in her life. Tonight she even had on blue jeans, and no one but Indiana would realize that the teal mohair jacket she wore had cost over nine hundred dollars. Sylvia had features like her daughter, too snub to be pretty, but she was good with scarves, draping them dramatically on her shoulder or neckline, which had a way of convincing people she was a very beautiful woman. Or it might have been her hair, the shiny shoulder-length blond flow that tucked under at the ends with steely neatness, never showing the faintest outgrowth. Her careful makeup was tuned to the hour, the teal jacket, and the company. Christine had only to take one look at her to feel scrawny, straggly, and awkward.

The hug she gave Christine might have looked breezy and vivacious, but to Christine it had always felt as though she were being seized and rapidly rebuffed. Oh, she had spent years trying to straighten out her feelings about her mother. When her mother kissed Jesse hello, she reached up nervously to smooth his hair, which didn't need smoothing. It was her mother's most unnerving trait. She could pinpoint with breathtaking accuracy the areas where you were perfectly secure, and then undermine them with reassurances. The Ludans, of course, were fairly immune. As Indiana had once remarked, unless you made it a major project, you could only work emotionally stable people over if you started young enough.

In an unnecessary effort to set everyone at their ease,

Sylvia smiled at Jesse's mother, Mari. "Well, we've got our young idealist among us again. Did you know that Jesse was one of the cover stories for a leading news weekly in Tokyo? They ran a picture too. One of the surgeons from St. Mike's was on vacation and he sent it to us."

Jesse's aunt Rose said, "Then perhaps you'll give me a copy. I've been keeping a scrapbook—oh, you should see the things I've collected. Imagine seeing our little Jess in *Them* magazine as one of the fifty most intriguing men of the year."

Jesse shoved his hands in his pockets. Christine could almost feel his irritation heat the clearing. "Maybe I should hit the lecture circuit," he said sweetly.

His family, who understood him, turned up an array of grins, but her mother, who did not, said, "What an excellent idea! And I know just the agency to handle you. They did Connie Abbott after her first novel came out—they absolutely pamper you. It wouldn't be long at all before you had money for a new car."

Christine thought, What's wrong with our car? Aloud she said, "It was a joke, Mother."

Sylvia gave her a cool disciplining glance under a slightly uplifted brow. She hated to be wrong. "Well, perhaps now that the idea has been raised, you'll think it over." Then she turned aside and admired the evening, the Ludan grandchildren, and the mushrooms soaking in tubs of salt water.

Christine smiled as Jesse put his lips to her ear and said, "Don't even think it. There's nothing wrong with our car."

Frisbees sailed over the clearing until the sun disappeared. The children's game changed to red rover until the clearing grew quite dark, and, as flames from the camp fire tinged faces scarlet, shooting sparks into the black sky, they played kick-the-can. By then the camp tables sagged under the weight of picnic food and the morels had been sautéed in butter. The family gathered near the fire on folding chairs, logs, and blankets, and talked, as they did every year, about the mushrooms— how many there were, how good they tasted, who ate a lot, who didn't eat as many as last year, whether it was better to have them with wine or beer or brandy. The Ludan children and in-laws discovered early that statements like "I don't like mushrooms" accomplished nothing beyond making oneself a target for aggressive attempts to teach one to like mushrooms. What one had to say was "Mushrooms don't agree with me," with its delicate hint of dire biological consequences. Then you were inundated with sympathy, not mushrooms.

English and Hungarian blended in a pretty babble with the crickets and bullfrogs in chorus from the reeds. Christine loved the sound of Hungarian speech. Its melodious timbre came, Jesse said, from an unusually high proportion of long and short vowels to consonants. The younger kids wouldn't speak the language. It seemed to embarrass them, especially in front of their friends. If a parent or older relative spoke to them in Hungarian, they answered in English. Their father would shrug and say, "It's only natural."

One of Christine's favorite consequences of a two-culture family was the names. Depending on whether his name appeared in Hungarian or its English equivalent, or its formal or affectionate variation, Sandor could be Alexander, Sandy, or Sanyi. Andy could be Andrew, András, or Bandi. Of course, Jesse and Indiana were unique, the mistakes. They had immigrated to America with the Hungarian names Zsolt and Attila, and a social services worker, probably with visions of grade school recesses, had suggested that Janos change their names to something more American. His choices after three weeks of English classes showed just how difficult it was to come in cold to another culture. He'd picked Jesse from Jesse James, a frontier figure Americans seemed to venerate, and Indiana from a newspaper piece on the heroes of the Indianapolis 500, which Janos had gathered was an important patriotic battle. He still laughed sometimes at the image of himself naively naming his sons after an outlaw and a racetrack.

After dinner, the talk grew softer. Older folks settled down to tell stories, younger ones mingled. Sandor came by to drop a fresh beer bottle into Jesse's hand, patted his shoulder, and said, "Have a little brewski, Jess." Peter, the wild brother who'd grown up to be a rock promoter and own a penthouse overlooking the lake before his twenty-fifth birthday, had caught Jesse in a moment of reverie and made him laugh by playing a chorus of "Folsom Prison Blues" on the guitar. Sometimes a brother or a cousin or a sister would come up to Jesse and hug him for no reason at all. They knew, and they gave him what they could.

Christine had carried her pie plate back to the table and, standing with her back to it, she watched Jesse from a distance. He was making a miniature canoe in birch bark and twine for Nicky, explaining the steps as he worked, a touch of humor tugging at his shapely mouth. Firelight burnished his profile in warm red and gold tones. His face seemed more relaxed than it had been since the day he'd come home.

A soft maternal chuckle drew Christine's attention to Beth, who was sitting on a blanket with her head tucked into Sandor's shoulder. Her jacket was opened, and Sandor's hand rested against the rounded upper curve where her pregnancy pressed against her orange velour sweater. Sandy leaned forward to place a light kiss where his hand had been, and another kiss, gentle with relaxed eroticism, on her lips. Mesmerized by the tenderness between them, Christine followed the kiss in her mind until she became suddenly conscious that she was intruding on a very intimate moment and looked away, her cheeks smitten with color.

But Sandy missed very little, and before she could wander off, he called her. She turned.

"The baby's moving," he said. "Come and see."

Very embarrassed, but not unwilling, she came to the foot of the blanket and sat down on her heels. With placid kindness he stroked her chin, his smile radiating in creases from his eyes, and, taking hold of her wrist, he placed her palm on Beth's stomach.

"Up a little bit," Beth said, and his hand carried Christine's upward obediently. "Have you ever felt this before, Chris?"

"No," she said. Her eyes remained self-consciously on Sandy's strong fingers where they clasped her wrist, and she thought how strange it was that in a world full of humans she had never felt one move inside a mother. *"Oh.* Was that—"

"Yes." Beth leaned back contentedly.

Fascinated by the tiny life stirring under her hand, Christine said, "Does it hurt?"

"No. I like it." Catching Christine's smile as she looked

up, she said, "Are you afraid of going through all of this?"

"A little."

Beth nodded. "So was I. Before."

Jesse joined them, his hands falling on her shoulders, massaging contentment into her. He pulled her to her feet, bowing her lithe body to fit his, rocking her lightly and dipping his face to the side of her throat, tasting the little-girl saltiness of her skin. "One of these days soon," he whispered, "shall we start a baby together?"

She turned in his arms, burying her face in his sweater, and he felt her nose rub up and down on his chest as she nodded, and the lift of her taut cheek as she smiled.

Two logs away, watching them with a small glass of Hungarian apricot brandy in her hand, Sylvia Bell smiled and said, "Look at them, Mari. Aren't they sweet?"

Jesse's mother had been poking a wandering nut-brown lock back under her cotton head scarf. "They've been through a rough time, those two."

Christine knew her mother firmly believed that the rough time her daughter had been through resulted from having a husband who was too pigheaded for his own good.

"Well, they're two grown kids," Christine heard Sylvia say. "No one can tell them how to live their lives."

Janos Ludan leaned forward in his chair to pour her more brandy. "No. No one. He's a strong man, my Jesse."

"Stubborn." Christine's mother sipped her brandy. "Stubborn."

Jesse was watching now, and though Christine could feel his stillness, she knew he was too courteous to be provoked into an argument with someone like her mother, whom he considered a political lightweight, in the middle of a family picnic. On the other hand, last week he had told a soccer official to shove it. She was glad to see Indiana step his long legs over the log and sit down beside her mother. He said easily, "It's good to be stubborn."

"Sometimes," said Christine's mother. Christine knew her mother would have let it drop there because she hated overt public disagreements—*overt* being the operative word—and besides, she was a balletomane. Indiana Ludan was one of the few people with whom Christine had ever seen her mother become rather bashful. Her dad, however, was not so sensitive to social nuances.

"It's possible to be too determined," he said, clearing his throat. "Sometimes you have to bend. That's the way the world is. You have to make compromises."

Indy stretched his legs out before him with sinuous precision. "Don't you think, Dr. Bell, that there are certain compromises that would entail giving up one's self-respect?"

Christine saw that her mother was beginning to look disconcerted, as if she suspected someone of trying to miscast her as the villainess. "Don't misunderstand us, Indiana. No one is talking about not having ideals. Obviously we've raised Christine to have ideals or Jesse wouldn't have married her, isn't that right?"

"But when a judge orders you to reveal information, you should comply," Christine's father said. "That's the law."

Beth spoke up suddenly. "There used to be a law in England that you could be hanged for shooting the king's deer. That was the law; was it right?"

"If I lived in England and that was the law," Christine's mother said hotly, "I certainly wouldn't have shot one of the king's deer. That's precisely the point. When push comes to shove, you've got to bend. But here's Jesse thrown in jail with car thieves and"—she stopped, as if it was beyond her to imagine what sort of desperate characters her son-in-law had been exposed to—"and God knows what all, and left with a criminal record!"

It was dangerous to speak. Christine knew she was in an emotional state, but the words came unbidden. "Jesse doesn't have a criminal record, Mother. There were no criminal charges against him. It's insane that in a system of justice where murderers can demand a jury trial, one judge and one DA in some secret hearing can throw someone in jail without having to justify what they're doing to a soul."

"Now, that I never did understand," said her father, shaking his head.

"It shouldn't happen in America!" she cried in a breaking voice. Silence followed, sticky with its massed sympathy, and Christine realized that she had gone forward, and that she was alone without Jesse's touch in appalling exposure. But Jesse made no move to come to her. He must have realized it would have made her weep, and the small part of her that wasn't actively mortified was so pleased that he saw she could stand without a shield. Still, she was chokingly relieved when Jesse's grandmother ended the moment by hurrying forward and drawing out one of the linen handkerchiefs she embroidered so beautifully to press into Christine's hand.

"There, all of you. See what you do?" she demanded, rounding on her grandson. "Just like your father, you are, Jesse. Worrying about the government, and this idea and that, and your poor wife had such a sad face at

Christmas without you. Every month while you were away I sent money to the fathers at Holy Hill to say Mass for her, all alone in that big house without the love of a husband. You should worry about her now, instead of to think about politics."

Christine saw that her father had risen to his feet and put out his arms to her, this small man whom she felt she hardly knew, standing hesitantly. And then she was in his arms clinging to him, remembering the words she had listened to so lightly earlier: Jesse's mother saying, "Something good comes from everything." And she knew why Jesse had held back.

"Hey, you know what?" Janos Ludan was struggling to his feet, pulling himself up by his cane, speaking in a clear, carrying voice. "She's a special girl, my daughter-in-law. So many wouldn't have stood with my son. But Jesse knows about freedom because he learned from me. I love this country, and I pass that love on to my children, and I teach them about what happened to Hungary so they will never take freedom for granted. I want everyone here to *listen good*"—he drove his cane into the hard ground as though striking the words into stone— "to what I say when I tell them that my son Jesse told that judge to go to hell because I brought him up so that he doesn't know how to live another way but by his conscience. And I'm proud of him."

The wind made a nice sound through the trees; the fire crackled a warm tune. Rising slowly to his feet, Sandor joined his father.

"I propose a toast," he said, holding aloft his brandy glass. "To Jesse and Christine."

"Hear! Hear!" her father said, releasing her, helping her mother to stand as everyone was doing. And Jesse slid his hand in Christine's as the glasses raised to them sparkled in the firelight. "To Jesse and Christine," Janos Ludan repeated. "And to America!" They toasted. It was a beautiful moment, free from cynicism.

"To the brave Hungarian Freedom Fighters of 1956!" It was her father's voice.

There was a roar of approval. Janos drained his glass and reached out to pump her father's hand.

Indiana, with his sweeping smile, was putting a brandy into her hand, and one into Jesse's, and her husband was holding her in a wantonly loving gaze. He raised his glass toward her and murmured, "To Christine."

"To Jesse," she said, and kissed him.

That drew a delighted "Ahhhh!" from their combined families.

And Christine, who had endured being the center of attention for as long as it was humanly possible, extended her glass toward the dark sky and sang out, *"To the mushrooms!"*

chapter eight

Jesse hummed to himself on the long ride home. They pulled into the driveway under a silvery moon and the night song of crickets. It was unseasonably cool.

Thirty minutes later, Christine came out of the shower yawning, combing her fingers through her wet hair to separate the snarls. She considered her drawer of nightgowns and underclothes, looking for interesting possibilities, but when she dropped her bath towel the cool bedroom air nipped her moist skin, raising the flesh on her limbs and back. Abandoning the notion of becoming a siren, she slid into her washed-out cream-colored jeans and a cotton sweater of Jesse's.

Downstairs Jesse had made a fire. Fat knots from pine wood popped in the hearth, and he lay stretched out on the couch, his hair, loose and fluffy from an earlier shower, brushing against the persimmon country french floral

131

print beneath. One bare foot swung absently in its upraised posture over the back of the couch. He wore his oldest jeans and nothing else. He seemed warm and drowsy, an open issue of *Mother Jones* magazine on his thigh, staring in a stuporous way into the gray emanation from their twelve-inch black-and-white TV set which he'd placed on a side table beside her african violets.

Once upon a time, they had owned an eighteen-inch color television with a beautiful picture, but it had had a tendency to put Jesse into a trance, so she had convinced him to trade down to something less inviting. Small good it had done her. Jesse was gazing, enraptured, at a rerun of *Second City TV* as though he were trying to memorize the script. When she saw him like this, she could hardly resist the devilish urge to do something frightful to him, like putting crushed potato chips in his pants. Coming into the living room, she employed her most pleasant voice.

"It was really fun today."

No response, though the long, graceful fingers on the couch back lifted briefly in what might have been a greeting. A glance at the tube showed her that John Candy was in a restaurant skit. Someone had tossed a salad at him. Tough competition. She gave it another shot.

"I'm glad we went, aren't you?"

A suspenseful pause. Then, "Yeah..." he said, his eyes glued to the television.

In the same pleasant tone, she asked, "Have you got an erection?"

"Yeah..." His rapt gaze never left the screen. "It's immense."

That surprised a laugh from her. "You were listening after all."

"Did you expect less from one of the fifty most intriguing men of the year?" His light gaze touched her body. "Do you have anything on under your jeans?"

She pretended to be indignant. "I may, or I may not."

His smile began in his eyes, a slow translucent softening that reminded her of the glowing iridescence of a rainbow. He got up, flicked off the television, and sat back on the couch.

"Let's find out," he said. "C'mere and sit on me."

He drew her down, her knees straddling his thighs, her hands against his naked chest. "I don't want to take you away from your favorite pastime."

Stirring in soft circles over the upper curve of her thighs, his fingers were moving slowly inward. "Oh, I don't think you will."

"If you leave it on long enough"—she gestured to the TV, her breath halting just a little at his treatment of her legs—"cartoons come on at six in the morning."

"Why is it that whenever I let you convince me I'm a TV addict, I come home in the middle of the afternoon to find you watching ancient segments of *Green Acres?*"

"Rural humor has a strong historical tradition," she said primly, leaning her cheek against his collarbone, letting his chest warm her.

"Speaking of things sylvan, I wanted to let you know that I'm glad you bullied me out of staying home today."

"I didn't bully you." The crush of his shoulder on her cheek muffled her voice.

"You did. But I'm glad."

"You know you're fortunate to have a family that cares so much about you." She didn't like the slightly sad note in her voice. But it was there. "It's a head start on happiness."

His arms closed around her. "You have a lot from your parents too. It's just not as easy to see because they're not overtly..."

"—affectionate."

"I was going to say 'imperative.'"

"Hmmm. I've never seen your parents behave imperatively."

"No. You don't see it," he said. "But it's there. A set of standards that locks you into certain paths..."

She slid her arms around his neck. "What do you think I got from my mother?"

"Poise, and a strong sense of self. Sometimes her methods are a little inverted, which I don't think she can help. But here you are at twenty-six"—he gently squeezed her thigh—"muscles like a rock, character like a rock."

His words meant more to her than he could have known. "You think so? I thought you didn't like my mother."

"When she's unpleasant to you she's not high on my list. But every once in a while I get this vision that snaps open like a shutter and I see parts of you in her and it makes me like her more."

"Even after what she and Dad said about your decision to go to jail?"

"More than ever after that. What kind of parents would they be if they weren't mad at their daughter's husband for getting himself thrown into prison like a jackass?" His palms brought up her face. She was flushed, and the skin around her eyes had a pulled look, as it always did when she tried to talk about her mother. Yet she was smiling, and he wondered if it had anything to do with the moment when her mother had come to her as they were getting into their car. She had given Christine one of those careless embraces that made him want to take the woman aside and say, "For God's sake, touch her gently. She's strong, but she'll never be tough." And just as he was feeling that familiar zing of anger, Sylvia had said, "Christine, I wanted you to know. . . . I'm proud of you too." It was the first time he had ever heard her say anything like that to Christine.

He ran the back of his finger over her cheek. She was very warm.

"It's too hot by the fire for a sweater," he said. "Lift your arms."

"Ahem. You asked me what I have on underneath? Nothing."

His hands roved down over the sweater, tracing her firm muscles until he reached her back pockets. He spread his fingers there, cupping his hands full of her, and dragged her close to nuzzle his way under the big loose sweater. He felt her breath surge as his tongue wet her nipples and then left a light trail down her midriff before he emerged, his hair disheveled.

"You're right, you don't," he said, drawing up the sweater from the bottom. "God, I love marriage."

That was enough to make her put up her arms, her small breasts pointing upward, the nipples rosy-pink under the cotton caress of the rising sweater. When it was off, her hair was mussed too and she felt slightly giddy and alive, in love with the clean intoxication of the sensual intimacy. She wound closer to him, her legs curling into his, her head alight in the hard cradle of his arm. One of her breasts was squeezed into his side; the other, untrammeled and sprinkled with chestnut freckles, lay lightly against his chest. His skin was smooth and fresh beneath her lips, scented with the herbal pine warmth of the fire.

He had been waiting for her, marking time with television until she came, and now with her so close, like another part of himself, he looked wonderingly back on the weeks he had nervously anticipated this moment. Suddenly it was as if he had never been away, and this closeness felt so good, so right to him; and the thing he had thought was going to bring him wrenching agony, the opening of his damage to another human being, seemed only the simple and natural consequence of his love.

"Chris...there's something I'd like you to know." He felt her move slightly against him. She became alert as he continued. "I had a deeper reason for refusing to cooperate with the John Doe. Deeper as in more elusive. It's not something I can explain in a clear way, or lay out in a formula.... That's why I always talk like some damned pedant about principles and ethics, but that doesn't begin to touch the way I feel."

She was quiet. Then she nodded. "It has to do with Hungary, doesn't it?"

She knew. Of course she already knew. What a futile, foolish thing it had been to close himself to her.

"When I was in jail, these bits and pieces kept coming back to me—things I hadn't thought about in years. Kid's memories."

"Tell me."

He relaxed his head against the cushions, his hands winnowing her damp hair, watching the play of the hearth glow in it, letting the warmth of the fire take the wet darkness from it to reveal the scarlet highlights within.

"In 1956 we were in Budapest with my father. He

was a cavalry officer then, and we lived in this little apartment across from a park. Sandy used to walk me over to the duck pond, and we'd feed the baby ducks crumbs from our breakfast. And this one day, there was all this noise and excitement in the street and Sandy grabbed my hand and there was a huge...just a *huge* brown tank in the street." He hesitated, trying to capture that long-ago feeling. "I was only four at the time, so you can imagine how it looked to me.

"Anyway, my father and some other men were riding way on top of it and they were singing about freedom, something about whether we would be free men or slaves. All I thought was that it was exciting, like a holiday or something, and when I asked Sandy what was happening, he said that it was a Russian tank and that Father had taken it from them. I was about to ask him if that was going to make the Russians mad when I saw my father unfurl a Hungarian flag. It looked strange to me because it was the same flag I'd always seen, but this one didn't have the big red star in the middle. My mother had come out and she took me up in her arms—she was laughing and crying at the same time. I'd never seen anyone do that before. She said, 'Look at it, little one. It's the real flag of Hungary.'"

He drew a heavy breath and straightened his back. "She was still holding me when we heard this terrific roar. People started diving into doorways and screaming, and airplanes came roaring out of nowhere low over the rooftops, and you couldn't hear anything but this thundering noise. My parents tried to drag me inside but I was thinking—wow! airplanes!—you know, how a kid would, and I went running back outside again to look at them. My father came after me—it was the only time he ever struck me. All around us dust seemed to be exploding and our windows began to shatter, and—"

He took another powerful swallow of air. "Looking back, I realize that the planes were strafing the streets with machine-gun fire. When I went to the park again with Sandy, we found this tiny duckling under a bench, and it had been shot. I didn't really know what death was, but it was ugly. Very ugly. I asked Sandy what did this and he said the airplanes. The Russian MiGs. And in my little child's mind I was angry, Christine. I was so angry because I thought, Why did they kill the little duck? Years later, even when we were in Milwaukee, I would look up when I heard a jet and think, Is that a MiG? and feel the return of this terrible anger."

His voice trailed, as though the primitive force of his child's anger was beyond his power to describe, and Christine realized that she had enclosed him in her arms. Fear thrilled through her for the little boy he had been, and she said nothing, just held on. Presently he said, "Has this made any sense?"

"Yes."

"Can you see that what I did had nothing to do with— I don't know—political ideology, I suppose. I only went to defend one thing, and that was the right of people to express themselves without fear. Do you understand?"

"Yes. Because it's the only civilized way."

That simply, he felt himself shed a corner of that inner darkness. They had stared for a long time into the fire in loving silence before she said, "I've always wondered if you remember anything about crossing the border out of Hungary."

Scooping up her hair, spilling it through his fingers, he said, "It was late in the year, and we had to walk—

I've no idea how far. My mother was carrying Indy. My father carried me. The ground was dotted with land mines and they didn't dare put me down or I would have been all over the place. My poor parents. I was crying because I wanted to walk. Sandy was crying because he was tired of walking." He rubbed the back of Christine's neck with a broad palm. "See, there were people living along the border who were willing to make a little extra on the side helping refugees get across. We were supposed to go across in the back of a feed wagon under a blanket, and to keep quiet so we wouldn't alert the dogs and border patrols for ten miles around." He began to laugh. "My father gave us brandy. It was supposed to make us sleep. But we all got hiccups instead, and hiccuped our way over the border. We were bouncing around under the blanket like jumping beans."

She could feel the tension slip from him, washing away in the vacant air.

He went on. "In Austria we stayed in a refugee camp where we had to sleep on straw. That was great. Straw fights. My mother wrapped Indy in a white blanket, and when she tucked him to sleep in the straw, she said, 'See, doesn't he look like the Christ child escaping to Egypt?'" He smiled. "Not a very prophetic image, was it?" After a thoughtful silence, he added, "That's all. It doesn't change anything. I just wanted you to know."

She shifted to see his face and to let him see in hers everything that words were inadequate to express. *"Szerelem,"* she said, inexpertly using the Hungarian, and kissed him.

"I love you too, Christine." His hand wandered in a slow line up the length of her arm. "Say, what was all that about between you and Beth? When you had your heads together laughing while we were cooking mush-rooms?"

"Ah . . ." she said. "Your girl friend from Pulaski High."

"What girl friend?"

"Charlene Czerwinski." She rolled the name lovingly off her tongue. "The first girl in Milwaukee to come to school braless."

Jesse groaned.

Warming to the subject, she said, "And she wore tight fuzzy sweaters."

He collapsed sideways and hid his face under a pillow. "Stop torturing me. I'd forgotten the girl completely."

"And a good thing too!" She lifted one edge of the pillow. "Did you have sex with her?"

"No," was his muffled reply.

"I don't believe it."

"It's the truth," he said, emerging. "My dad took one look at her and put me on the pill."

She put her face nose to nose with his and pulled the pillow over them both, her slow-burning grin almost touching his. "I'll bet you lost your virginity to Charlene Czerwinski."

"I've told you, I was a good Catholic boy until I got to college. My father said that we could make up our own minds once we were of age, but until then we had to go by the rule. Same rule for boys and girls."

"What was it?"

"That we could do anything we wanted on a date, above the waist or below—"

"Heavens!"

"*But* we couldn't unfasten our jeans."

"Really?" The sensual smile spread wider.

"Really. I thought you knew about that rule. From

the state you were in the first time we made love, I thought you were a staunch practitioner of it."

The pillow was quickly transformed into a weapon as she took it up and began pummeling him with it. "Oh, a comedian, eh? Eat feathers, Hungarian meatball! How would you like to be reduced to a pot of goulash?"

He twisted the pillow from her grip and stuffed it back under his head. Catching her waist in both hands, he moved so that her thighs spanned his hips, and as that part of her was gliding over his pelvis, she felt the insistent sting of her own desire. Love tingles swept upward in her spine and her lips began to respond with a pouting rush of erotic pressure.

With a pounding heart, she asked, "Am I being treated to your old high school technique?"

"It's improved a little since then."

"Says you." She knew her lucent, fluid gaze was telling him everything.

"Never doubt it." His fingertips were kneading her inner thighs, tracing over the seams, creating ravishing sensations inside her jellied nerve endings. "Follow my father's rule," he breathed, "and you learn all kinds of things about how to achieve ecstasy in denim." He slid his palm upward slightly, pressing in a slow circle, fanning his fingers, lifting very gently into her. The hot, pulpy feeling rising in her chest made her breath increasingly shallow.

"Somehow," she whispered, "I think Charlene Czerwinski had a much better time in high school than I did."

His hands left her burning thighs, skimmed her sides, and then let the erect tips of her breasts make a fiercely exciting caress down his fingers and palm as he lifted his hands to her hair. He held her head in a light grasp, watching her mouth as he drew her closer to receive his open kiss.

"With you," he said softly, "it's always been different." He pressed his mouth to her moist parted lips. "This means I love you." His mouth trailed to her throat. "And this means I love you. And this..." His voice faded to a whisper, more breath than sound, and she felt the tip of his tongue probe her nipple, and then his lips lightly tugging. His hands were kneading her shoulders as he pulled her closer, and her heartbeat capered in her throat. She held him to her, transported with sensual reverence, her hands in his thick hair.

"And this means what?" Her words were a shiver.

Huskily he said, "It means you're about to get yours, kid."

She started to say, "I've been wanting to get mine all day," but the words were lost in the tangle of her leaping senses. His hands were strong and steadying on her hips, supporting her so that his kisses could stroke down the muscular curve of her stomach. He shifted, laying her beside him, and the pressure of his mouth continued over her waist, over the denim, and down. She was lost in love, in the spinning sensations he was building in her, her hands working into his hair, her tingling fingers flexing through its flood of warmth. And then she was beneath him, his hands briefly touching the snap of her jeans, and she felt the wonderfully liberating wave of her zipper being gently lowered, and the soft, loving movements of his lips and tongue over the sensitive, quivery skin beneath. She felt her jeans falling away drawn down by him with all the naturalness of a spring breeze drawing at a flower petal. He laid her back on the cushion of her hair, and she gloried in the touch of his hands and his lips, melting for him, making it easy for him; and his slow coming into her was blindingly diffuse, a sweet stage-by-stage slipping into the grip of a dream—two become one, one heart, one body....

When at last they slept, they were twined together on the tumbled cushions, sharing the same pillow.

chapter nine

In the morning, after Jesse went off to watch the governor meet the first-shift workers at a meat-packing plant in Milwaukee's Menomonee Valley, Christine realized that she wasn't going to spend another night without him in their bed. Last night he had slept soundly on the cushions beside her. Perhaps the insomnia was over, perhaps it would return. Either way she wanted to face it with him. She had been alone too long.

She might simply have told him, "Tonight you're in with me, Ludan." But the giddy joy of their night together clung to her, making her think of all kinds of silly ways to tell him. Driving home in the afternoon after a day of dance classes, she wondered if he wasn't planning ways of telling her too. She stood in the spare room staring at the extra bed. It needed something. A boarder? A fifty-foot python? Dramatic gestures. Funniness. Laughing softly to herself, she found her upholstery needle and nylon thread and spent the rest of the afternoon hovering over the bed sewing spread to sheets to mattress in so many places that sleeping in that bed was not something anyone was going to be doing for a long time.

She had just emerged from the shower in a peacock-blue bath towel, feeling wily and festive, when she heard Jesse's car in the garage. She made it downstairs in time to see the front door fly open as if pushed by a mighty wind, and Jesse stalked in, slamming the door behind him. His jacket sailed across the room in a ball of cloth that toppled a lamp before coming to rest in a corner, and he threw himself down full length on the couch, one hand over his eyes. Standing still, feeling like a fool in her towel and her descending exhilaration, she said, "So how was your day, dear?"

Jesse lay quietly, trying to control his chattering tension, trying to push aside the curtain of blackness that had descended after the strained discussion with his editor this afternoon, when his unformed worries about what they intended to do with his career had become fact. Now he wished he didn't know. He wished he could go back to his springtime morning mood, because another day without this crazed stress would have been so good for him. And for her. He could practically taste the uncertainty in her voice as she said, "Do you think—are you coming down with something?"

"Terminal irritation. Tell me something, Chrissie. Why is the world so screwed up?"

"Maybe the world didn't eat a balanced breakfast."

"That's it. The four food groups..."

Silence reigned. She noticed his fist, trailing on the carpet fringe, clenching and unclenching.

"Do you want to talk about it?" she said finally.

"No. This may sound a little juvenile, but I want to tear the living room apart."

"Would you mind starting with the recliner? It's reminded me of a dentist's chair since the day we brought it home."

More silence. Then, through tight jaws, he said, "We've got that damned awards dinner tonight."

It was no secret to her that he wasn't looking forward to receiving the adulation of his peers. To him it meant the raising of a simple act of conviction into a glamorous sham. She thought, God, he's complicated. All of a sudden she felt rather exhausted. Trying to stifle the peevish resentment that was nibbling in an embarrassing way at her temper, she went over to pick up the lamp, watching him light a cigarette, drinking the smoke as though it were a fluid. The way he held the cigarette cupped into his palm reminded her that, however pervasive the influence of his family had been, he had spent much of his adolescence in the company of some very tough folks.

"The awards dinner is your place in the sun," she said. "You've earned it."

"My place in the sun . . ." He repeated the phrase as though he was getting some private satisfaction from disliking it. "It came right out of your skin, didn't it?" He sat up, regarding her with a straight look of startling brilliance. "Does some ephemeral honor make up for the days you've spent alone, for all the leaky faucets and broken garbage disposals and the terrible anxiety? Does it make up for the threatening letters?"

New life quickened her resentment. The last thing she needed was for him to have heard about the letters. "Who told you we got threatening letters?"

"My grandmother. It slipped out. Apparently she forgot I wasn't supposed to know. So I phoned my father about it this afternoon. I can hardly believe you've been keeping something like that from me. What if something had happened to you? What if one of those maniacs who wrote those letters had decided to attack you? Do you know what I've been doing on the way home? Counting the ways someone could get into this house."

"Don't worry," she said. "I slept with a bazooka."

He just stared at her.

"Look, you know what a chicken I am," she said. "Do you think I'd take any risks? Sandy wired the doors and windows with an intrusion warning device. You never saw it because I made him remove it when we heard you'd be out any day. And you will note he put deadbolts on the doors. Furthermore, there are neighbors on every side who knew what was happening, and the phones have one-touch dialing to the precinct number."

He was standing, shaking his head, his fear turning over and over inside him. Quietly he said, "Someone could have been waiting for you in the garage."

Her mind called up the image of those stark winter nights, hushed and frozen, when the darkness fell early; of herself driving alone and tired into the black crater of their garage.

"You could have been beaten." The wide line of his lips had paled. "You could have been raped."

He'd spent years as a court reporter, watching the shattered victims of assault give their heart-racking testimony on witness stands. Some nights he had come home harrowed, unable to make love to her. And she knew that the anger and blame that stood out tautly in his face was directed inward. But the lacerated heat of it seemed to flow from his eyes into her, and suddenly the weight was too much. She felt her own needs thrust against it, thrusting upward, rejecting it. For six months she had spent every waking moment in a terrible dread for his safety. Didn't he realize that?

"*You* could have been raped!" The words spilled out of her.

His lips parted in a hiss of exhalation, and he gave her a surprised look and then started to laugh with bitter hilarity. "Don't worry," he said. "My virtue is intact." He sat back down, his eyes closing. She could mark each breath by the uneven rise and fall of his chest. "My virtue is intact, if nothing else. Don't pay any attention to me. I'm not myself . . ." Jesus, he thought, what have I said to her? That she could have been raped in her garage. What a hideous thing to say to a woman.

He opened his eyes on her, standing icy-cold, straight as a rocket in her towel, the frigid rage in her horizon-blue gaze wrapping all of her in a kind of insistent dignity.

"It's too bad something didn't happen to me," she said. "Then I'd be the one with the permission to act so shattered."

She turned from him and ran upstairs, whacking the bedroom door closed behind her. The sound reverberated with a snap somewhere inside him; it was like being struck awake. He found himself admiring her exit, even as he regretted having been the cause of it. Smoking, hunching his shoulders back against the couch, he tried to bring some objectivity to the wreckage of his emotions. I'm acting like a kid, he thought. Why am I acting like a kid? What the world didn't need was to stop revolving on its axis because he was tense.

"Christine, I'm sorry," he shouted.

The bedroom door opened momentarily. "I don't accept apologies that are bellowed up the stairs."

In the bedroom he found her sitting in front of the mirror sticking hot curlers into her hair with shaking fingers. He leaned on the doorjamb.

"I'm sorry," he said.

She picked up a roller. One finger slipped from its spine into the hot inside and got burned. She dropped the curler, picked it up again, and rolled it furiously into her hair.

"Ouch. Damn. I don't know what you're apologizing for."

"For dumping my day in your lap. For yelling at you about not telling me you were getting those letters. If the situation had been reversed, I wouldn't have told you either."

He got rid of his cigarette and stood watching her, becoming increasingly enchanted by the graceful domesticity of being alone with her like this in marital intimacy.

She was taking out the rollers when she said, "There's something else, isn't there? Besides the letters."

"Work problems. Can we talk about it later?"

"That depends. Do you still want to tear the living room apart?"

As she lifted her hands to brush her hair, the light movement pressed her breasts upward to swell against the towel. The ends of her curls floated on her bare shoulders, and he imagined how they would feel against his face.

"No. I want to tear the towel away from your body."

She put her elbow on the dresser and stuck her chin into her palms. "I should roll my hair more often."

"It must be my proletarian upbringing. A woman in hair rollers does something to my libido."

Watching him cross the room slowly toward her, she took a long keen breath and said, "My mother always did say that if you were going to let a man see you in curlers, you might as well invite him into your bedroom."

His hands fell on the towel, gently gripping it, gently lowering it. "Then," he said, "we don't want to disappoint Mother."

The Milwaukee Press Club had always intrigued Christine. It had an atmosphere of worn gentility, the rooms shabby and aging but cozy, like a second-rate men's club fallen on hard times. Jesse said it reminded him of the visiting parlor in a rest home for destitute English lords. Green chalkboards covered the walls, with their marvelous dated autographs of past visitors: "Charles Lindbergh Aug. 20th, 1927"; "Lillian Russell 2/8/1916"; "Woodrow Wilson 17 Nov. 1910"; "Walter Cronkite April 13, 1975." Scattered in strategic places between the chalkboards were bulletin boards bearing the house rules and long lists of club members who were behind in their dues. Defiantly anachronistic and rarely polished brass spittoons were scattered here and there on the darkly patterned carpeting, mercifully holding nothing more revolting than an occasional gum wrapper.

But the bar was well stocked, and although the upright piano might have been much scarred with cigarette burns, it was in perfect tune. The nude over the bar was life-sized and had obviously shed her clothes a lifetime before anyone had thought of aerobic dancing or diet soda. The pink hue of her skin and her smile shared the same shameless radiance.

The rooms were packed for the awards dinner and bubbled with the sounds of friendly argument and hearty drinking. Streamers of pipe and cigarette smoke hovered at eye level like an acrid early morning mist. Jesse and Christine paused in the entrance hall, taking off their coats. He eyed the list of delinquent dues payers that fluttered there and saw his own name. "Gimme a break." He gestured at the list in exasperation. "Don't they read the papers around here? I've been in jail!"

Leaving Chris visiting with the *Journal* dance critic, he went off to bring himself up to date with old Louie, the manager, who wore a green eyeshade. The small, untidy office was empty and he was wondering whether to wait a minute when Angela Currie whisked into the room behind him. Before he could avoid it, she slid her arms around his neck and kissed him.

"Congratulations!" she said.

He disengaged himself quickly. It was clear she had more on her mind that congratulating him on the award he was going to receive. The kiss had been serious, and she had closed the office door—and she had tried this once before. She was the news director for the city's largest AM radio station, and he had been booked into a room in the same hotel as she had when they were covering the state Republican convention last year. She had asked him to come to her room on the pretense of a jammed suitcase, and while he'd been suspicious, he'd gone because she was probably telling the truth, and what if she was and he didn't help her? There was a formal reception in two hours that the press had been invitied to attend. Taken again. There had been no jammed suitcase and, as soon as he was in the room, she'd put herself into his arms and lifted his hand to her breast.

It was a very nice breast, but it had done absolutely nothing for him, beyond the faint surprise that people actually did things like that in real life. Now, looking through the transparent chiffon dress that was tilting off her shoulders, he was experiencing the feeling of a kid munching popcorn in the front row of a movie theater and going *"ugh"* when people kissed. Strange flesh.

"Am I a scalp to you, or what?" he asked.

She looked up at him with dark, delicious eyes. "When you say things like that, it makes me wonder whether you know how attractive you are. We're adults, right? Please take that moralistic look off your face; I'm not doing this because I'm out to get Christine. This has nothing to do with her. I only wanted you to know that I realize you're going through a high stress time, and if you're having trouble with Christine, I'm willing to be company. If you look on that as cheap sex, fine. I think that's nonsense, but I can handle it."

He felt a flicker of amusement as he thought, The trouble I'm having with Chris now is nothing compared to the trouble I'd be having with her if I laid you, kiddo. "Angie, think about it a minute. Am I shy?"

She didn't need a minute. "No."

"That's right, I'm not. So I don't have to be nudged into anything. I don't want to, and that's not going to change. I love Chris. She's the only woman I desire. And even if she weren't, I wouldn't do anything behind her back. You know what else? You're too smart to go around being outside action for some married guy."

She slung her long black hair with impatient disap-

pointment and a dark-eyed hurt that she did a credible
job of disguising under a faint wry grin.

"Well, all right," she said. "Man of steel. I leave for
the last time with my tail between my legs. Tell me one
thing. Does she realize what she's got in you?"

He was spared giving an answer by Christine, who
walked straight in and gave them both a startled look.
Angela stared back with reddened cheeks and brushed
past her.

Christine watched the lovely retreating figure and then
turned back to Jesse. "Now what? The old suitcase trick?"

"Yep."

"Honest to Pete." She grabbed a Kleenex from the
box on the desk and began to scrub the wine-toned lip
gloss off his mouth. "That woman. I'm going to have to
get you a can of Mace."

They both expected to be upset by the incident. Instead
it pulled them closer. He had been honest; she had had
complete faith. The base of love they had made together
was working.

In the club room they were met with a burst of greet-
ings and gaiety. Drinks were waiting for them on the bar
and Jesse stood with his arm on her shoulder and a scotch
in his hand as they were surrounded by well-wishers.
Shoptalk and affable gossip moved into teasing. In half
an hour everyone within a twenty-foot radius was en-
grossed in a humorous argument about whether the nude
should go. Jesse had sportingly ranged himself on the
side of the feminists, who wanted to take it down. The
man had a penchant for losing battles. Christine left for
the powder room just as someone was proposing keeping
the young lady and adding a male nude on the opposite
wall.

When she found herself combing her hair in the mirror with Angela Currie and the anchorwoman from channel nine news, she was almost relieved to get this first meeting over with. Her color was high. So was Angela's as she said, "He tells you everything, doesn't he?"

"No. But he tries to."

Angela snapped her purse closed and looked directly at her. "I think he's a wonderful man." Tightly she added, "You don't have to worry about me."

For once, Christine was grateful for her mother's training, which enabled her to have the gallantry not to say, "I wasn't."

She was on her way back to Jesse when his editor, Phil Jackson, separated himself from the snarl of newspeople by the piano. During Jesse's months of confinement, she had grown close to Phil in shared anxiety, and she returned his quick bear hug with pleasure. She was fond of him, in spite of what Jesse said about Phil's more-Lou-Grant-than-thou attitude.

There was one more wrinkle than usual in Phil's brow as he said, "I just got here, so I haven't seen Jesse yet. How is he?"

Concern was written all over him. Christine's antennae went up. "He's fine, Phil," she said cautiously.

He was trying unsuccessfully to get his pipe started, puffing vigorously. "Thank God for that. I can't tell you how sorry I am that he found out today. I didn't want to tell him at least until after the awards, but you know how he is. He got sick of hearing no, and I couldn't put him off any longer."

Tell him what? Work problems, she thought. Obviously it had been bad news. Surely they wouldn't have fired him. Salary cut? The paper was going under? Abstractedly she said, "I'm sure he understood."

Jackson put up his eyebrows and stuck his lighter back into the pipe. "You think so?" he said glumly. "He threw a paperweight through my window. Well"—he sighed —"tonight will help."

At the banquet, anyone watching would have thought-that, indeed, it was helping, but Christine knew Jesse's company manners when she saw them. He was uncomfortable. As the speeches singing his praises began, she put a hand on his arm and found that his forearm was rigidly tight.

Her gaze wandered back to the podium and above, to the elaborately carved wall niche above the speaker where the club mascot and namesake of Jesse's award reposed. The Sacred Cat. It was the press club's highest honor and it had gone in the past to some of the most illustrious names in journalism. The cat itself was the leathery remains of a once-living creature frozen in an animated posture, one paw upraised dramatically, yellow glass eyes glittering. To ask a club member why such a grisly object had been chosen as the club's symbol was to be told the story of how the poor creature's mummified remains had been discovered inside a hollow wall of the old press club after it had burned down at the turn of the century. "Yes," you could say, "but *why* was it chosen as the club's symbol?" And all you would hear was a repeat of the same story of how the cat had been found when they tore down the old clubhouse. Somewhere down the line the cat had been wired for sound—a speaker inside the mummy was attached to a mike in the manager's office, and old Louie with the green eyeshade would make it talk or sing or exhort the members to pay their dues. Jesse told her she shouldn't waste her time figuring it out. Journalists often had a streak of warped humor.

The speeches continued, and she could almost hear Jesse thinking that words and phrases like courage, sacrifice, and upholding the great tradition of a free press were going for a dime a dozen. But she was beginning to bathe in the applause, the tributes to Jesse's integrity, the frequent mention of herself—except that it was a long time to be under all eyes and to try not to drip anything on herself or scratch her head. Or to cry, when Phil Jackson presented Jesse's award with an emotional speech and wet eyes.

Afterward she walked to the car with Jesse through the warm, muggy night. The starlings were calling.

"What a circus," Jesse said. But his inflection was more affectionate than sarcastic. Christine felt herself relax. City lights faded the sky to the color of maple syrup. The streets were almost free of traffic at this hour in this part of the city, and the shop awnings flapped in a damp, peppery lake breeze. In the quiet, Christine heard the distant clank and muffled chugging of the Milwaukee Road rail yards, which never slept. She reached in her purse for the car keys and felt the Sacred Cat award, cold and solid in her purse in its wrapping of tissue paper.

Jesse reached for a cigarette from his pack. Hello, crutch. Intercepting a wifely glance from Christine, he said, "I need it."

She put her hand to her jaw, rubbing muscles that ached from smiling. "You *think* you need it."

He stopped and replaced her fingers with his own, running his fingertips lightly up and down her jaw in a soft massage, smiling. "Is that any way to talk to a hero? Didn't you listen to the speeches. I can do no wrong."

She pulled his arm behind her shoulder and began to walk again, holding his long straight fingers in her hands, polishing his wedding band with her fingertip. How she loved him—this entrancing Don Quixote of a man who thought he was nothing special for living to his principles. She remembered suddenly the many times and small ways she had tried to protect him. Not once had it been necessary. His spirit had sunlight all through it. The moods and the temper that chewed things to bits were nothing, the surface aftershocks of fatigue. Jesse, I understand now. I'd only forgotten in six months how very strong you are. Her fingers tightened on his.

"Does throwing a paperweight through your editor's window qualify as doing no wrong?" she asked.

"Is that what Phil told you? For God's sake, I was gesturing. It slipped. Wouldn't you know it, the thing sailed out the open window and landed on Estlund's Oldsmobile."

"Estlund! You mean your publisher's car?"

"His wife's. I've never been more embarrassed in my life. It left a dent the size of a basketball. Now Jackson's convinced I'm a hothead. Did he tell you what they've decided to do with me?"

"No. I want to hear it from you."

He took a deep drag on his cigarette. A cherry glow from the brightening ash lit his strained features. "Chris, they've reassigned my court beat."

She halted. "What?"

The green eyes looked down into hers as if they were searching for something there to hold on to. "They've given my beat to someone else. Just like that. *Fini.* The DA who sent me up was promoted to head of the Felony

Unit, and they've decided at the paper that if I cover any cases my credibility will be open to question." The bleak irony of it showed in his voice. He had gone to prison to defend his public voice in the courts. And in the end, it was to be silenced anyway.

She stood without moving, letting him find comfort in her eyes as long as he needed it. Then she said, "Isn't there anything we can do?"

"Whatever there was to do I did this afternoon. They're not going to change their minds. If I did a column with even a hint of criticism about the DA's office, all the DA would have to do is hold a press conference and say, 'Hey, bull, Ludan's got a grudge.' The public wouldn't know who to believe."

With her heart pouring out to him, she released one hand from his fingers and slid it around his waist, holding the taut flesh in a hard embrace.

"What will you do now?"

"The opinion column, I guess. They want to step it up to a daily and move it from the features section to the editorial page, and the front page on Sundays. Phil was making noises about working it into syndication, but I don't know if anything will come of that."

"What? But Jesse, that's wonderful."

His cheek came to rest wearily on her hair. "Maybe tomorrow I'll see that. Today it feels like a payoff, babe. If I was going to move along to something else, I didn't want it to happen like this."

"I know."

She twisted in his arms, stretching on tiptoe to reach his face, touching her lips to his mouth. At first he could not seem to respond, but in a minute she felt his lips grow warmer and begin to move. She dragged her tongue along the tip of his lower lip and gently teased his mouth open.

"If you're trying to console me," he whispered, "it's working." And he took her by the shoulders and propelled her lightly backward against the red brick wall they were passing. "Try this one for size." The kiss he gave her was a sudden deep one, and at first she was unable to acquit him of indulging in comedic excesses. But something about the way he pressed his hard thigh into her, and the way his hand in her hair forced her head back and her mouth up to his turned her laughing protest into an unexpected moan of pleasure.

While they kissed, she ran her hands over his back and shoulders and nape, entranced suddenly with this new untamed behavior in him. She was no longer afraid of this short-fused and highly charged side, because it was only the energy he had always had, burning ever brighter. And this kiss—it was *very* exciting, and she knew her lips would be sore afterward, but she also remembered the long, languorous kisses they used to indulge in at odd moments like this. It was as though he were on a high-speed treadmill, trying to make up for time lost over the past six months. And there was his anger—that was it. It was anger that transformed him, real anger with real objects that couldn't be attacked. The judge, his editor, the iron bars that had held him trapped away from her, and the no-less-real bars of his own idealism, which had driven him into jail—these were the sources of his anger, all of them unreachable. She broke the kiss.

"Jesse," she breathed. "I know just what you need."

"Yeah, so do I," he said, and began to kiss her again.

She pressed her hand on his chest and pulled his wrist. "Come to the car," she said, smiling.

"If I do, will you engage in outlawed sexual practices with me under the hatchback?"

She was laughing as she unlocked the car and opened the passenger door for him. "Don't get your hopes up, tiger, I have something else in mind." She pulled the car out into the empty dark street, zooming through a traffic light as it turned yellow.

"I hope you're taking me someplace to molest me," he crooned, running a fingertip down her bare arm.

"Stop it; you'll make me have an accident. How can I properly brake and shift with weak knees? You'll get what you need."

He watched her turn the car onto the freeway ramp under the Life Saver-orange glow of streetlights. "Where to?"

"I found this neat little amusement park last month when I was out shopping . . ."

"Isn't it kind of late for miniature golf?"

"What's the matter?" She gave him a hooker's wink. "Don't you want to make a hole in one?"

"You poor fallen preppie," he said, beginning to catch the jumpy, playful quality of her mood, beginning to awaken to the night, to the sight and nearness of her. "You married a guy from the ethnic ghetto and got earthy. Are we going to drive go-carts?"

"Stop guessing. We'll be there soon enough." She rolled her window down, letting the velvet night wind toss her hair. The sounds of crickets rose and fell as they passed the increasingly open spaces between houses and shopping centers, and she remembered her father saying once that this part of town had been considered country about the time she was born. After a minor traffic tangle caused by the ending of a drive-in movie, she turned the car into the parking lot of the amusement park.

"Bozo's Amusements," he read aloud. "Open All Night. You're taking me to meet Bozo."

She parked the car, went to the passenger side, grabbed him by the shoulder, and pulled him out with all the forcefulness she could muster. Then, firmly gripping his arm, she led him to the change counter and handed the bald yawning man in a Hawaiian shirt a five-dollar bill. "Quarters please." Then she led her husband past the miniature golf, where a small group of teenagers played, past the idle shadowed go-carts to a net-shrouded paved area about the size of a tennis court.

"The batting machine!" he said, comprehension dawning.

She laughed at the interest in his eyes, tickled to have surprised him. "Whale away for a while and see what that does for you," she suggested.

It was eleven o'clock at night, and he had been through a long, difficult day. But he was so high wired from it that he was relieved to shed his jacket into her arms and head for the fast-ball cage, rolling up his sleeves.

"This might not be as therapeutic as you think," he said. "I never shone in baseball."

She rested her back against a metal support and said encouragingly, "Go on. Pound that horsehide." She grinned, watching him assume a professional-looking stance that belied his disclaimers, and fed three quarters into the metal box that hung outside the cage. She wondered who he was facing with that bat as the mechanical arm at the end of the cage began to turn slowly. Whom did he see right now? The judge? Phil Jackson? The mechanical arm scooped a ball from the rain-gutterlike trough and shot it like a cannonball at Jesse. It came so fast that Christine cried out involuntarily. Before the words left her mouth, Jesse's bat connected with the ball and sent it rocketing back into the net, which bellied and whipped.

"There you go," she called. "Hungarians can play baseball too."

But when the next ball came whizzing by six inches from his face, he grinned back at her and said, "Somewhat."

Twenty minutes later, beginning to hit his stride, ready for more quarters, he looked around for Christine and saw her in the medium cage, flailing away with occasional success. She had taken off her heels, and her feet in their light stockings were braced apart on the concrete. Her black silky dress had a halter neckline and no back down to her freckled waist, which meant she had little enough on underneath to show him the clear outline of her body as she moved. Fascinated, he watched her small, delicate breasts bounce a half beat behind her swing, and all thoughts of extra quarters went out of his head.

He put his shoulder against the metal-pipe door frame of her cage and gave her a soft version of a street-corner wolf whistle.

She turned, treating him to the smile in her Hayley Mills eyes. "Isn't this great?" She sounded winded.

He pushed himself off the frame and came toward her.

"Hello, there, young lady," he said. "We haven't been introduced"—he put his arm around her naked back—"but I'm a talent scout for the Milwaukee Brewers, and with an arm like yours"—his fingers explored it—"I think we could use you as a designated hitter." He began walking with her toward the car, past the man in the Hawaiian shirt, who was dozing behind his counter. A cloud of moths fluttered in a spotlight. "Someone with your batting eye is wasted on a two-bit batting machine, you know what I mean?"

He slid her into the car beside him and drew her willing sweetness into his arms. Between a set of electric twining kisses he murmured, "Let this be a lesson to you, my little Mickey Mantle. Never listen to the promises of a talent agent."

"Oh, I don't know, coach," she whispered back. "I've already made it to first base."

chapter ten

She fell heavily asleep on the way home, nodding against his shoulder. Gazing down at her tenderly when he stopped at a red light, he tucked back a hair that had strayed to cling to the softly shining moisture on her lips. She's worn out, he thought. I've been running her around in circles. Have I always been this intense? What tricks have I forgotten that I used to know to get rid of tension? Peace of mind—it was a delicate balance that seemed so simple until it faltered, and then it became an intricate maze of interwoven parts, a philosophical journey through any number of locked doors. Forget a few keys and you can be in real trouble. We're finding our way back, Christine.

He carried her up to the house for the simple pleasure of feeling the weight of her press into his arms. They moved from the balmy night into the quiet house, her head against his chest, her swirling curls tickling his chin. The dim ivory light from the street lamp on the corner reached through the window and fell over his shoulder, illuminating the powdering of freckles on her nose, and he brushed the spot with his lips.

Her lips parted. Her lashes fluttered. "I love it when you heft me around like Tarzan," she murmured. "Are you still going to do this when you're sixty?"

"From vine to vine, with you over my shoulder," he promised, and softly pushed open the bedroom door with his foot, spiriting her to the bed, trying to lay her down like a magic carpet landing.

Her lips opened just enough to say, "Am I pretty?"

Pulling off her shoes, he answered, "You're beautiful."

"Most beautiful woman in America?"

Searching lightly, he found and retrieved the gold ornament from her hair and her French earrings.

"In the world," he told her softly.

He pulled the summer cover up and tucked it around her neck. "I love you, Chris." He kissed her lips and left.

She rolled on her side, curling up, with a light wisp of regret. She'd wanted to seduce him, but she'd simply been too sleepy. It was wonderful to be taken care of like this. No, she thought drowsily, he can't go back to sleeping in the other room. Then she remembered. He literally couldn't go back to sleeping in the other room. This afternoon, which seemed like a lifetime ago, she had sewn his bed into one piece. The memory shocked her awake like a pitcher of cold water. Vaulting up, running across the hall, she arrived in his doorway to find him staring in a very peculiar way at the bed.

He tugged at the pillow. It was solid. He tugged at the base of the spread. Solid. A smile hovered. "What did you do to it?"

"I sewed it together with an upholstery needle."

His arms folded around her. "Christine . . . the dreams are less vivid now, but I'm still restless. I wake up a lot. Do you think you'll be able to—"

The phone rang.

"I'm going to break that thing into a thousand little pieces," Jesse said pleasantly.

Giving him a big sleepy squeeze, she thought, It doesn't matter. This is marriage. We'll both be here later.

She picked up the phone in their bedroom, answering it with the noncommittal hello she'd learned to use while Jesse was gone.

The voice on the phone said, "Hello? Uh . . . is Jesse Ludan there?" It was a young male voice afflicted with a startled hesitation. "I mean—is this the right number for him?"

She tried to pull up an identity: nervous young male, indifferent telephone manners. No, she didn't recognize the voice. Cautiously, because Jesse could get some strange calls, she said, "This is the right number. May I tell him who's calling, please?"

"Oh . . . uh, sure. This is . . . er, a friend of his. Well, not a friend, exactly. He used to know me. Listen, is he sleeping or something? I mean, I'm really sorry. I can call back later. Like when the sun comes up, I mean. Look, never mind." Then the hesitant voice changed, as though he'd seen a vision. "Say, you must be his wife, Christine." He said her name with reverent awe, as if she were Joan of Arc. She couldn't resist the inadvertent homage. Jesse was in the doorway making a thumbs-down hang-up motion, but the voice on the phone sounded like someone who needed pity.

"No, you didn't disturb anything. Hold on. I'll get him for you," she said, stimulating Jesse into another exasperated dismissive motion. She covered the receiver and said in a stage whisper, "It's, uh, someone who's your friend . . . er, well, not exactly your friend, but, uh, you knew him once."

That didn't seem to identify the caller to Jesse. He rolled his eyes and took the phone with a terse, "Yeah."

She watched him curiously as he listened to thirty seconds of what she strongly suspected was apologies from the caller. Finally Jesse seemed to home in on the caller's identity.

"No, it's all right, Max. I'm glad you called." His voice was perfectly polite, but his face was a comic mask of annoyance, the look she knew was always an equal mixture of playacting and real irritation. He listened again.

"I'm really sorry to hear that. What a tough break," Jesse said finally. More listening. "Sure we can talk. What about tomorrow?" His look of comic exasperation deepened. "You're where?" Jesse sank to the bed, covering the receiver and emitting a long sigh, a smile quirking his lip. "No, no," he said, obviously interrupting further apologies. "Why don't you come on over now? Now, it's fine, really. She'll be delighted to meet you. She loves late-night company. No, really, we were just sitting around watching the *Late Late Show*. Yeah, that's right, with Dr. Cadaverino. Right, fine, five minutes. See you then." He hung up and flopped back on the bed.

"Who's this company I'm supposed to meet at a time when most decent people are fast asleep?" she demanded.

"Ohh, he's this"—he waved his hand aimlessly—

"this kid . . . who was in my cell block. I told him—unwisely, I guess—that he could call me when he got out if he needed somebody to talk to. He's coming over."

"Here?" she squeaked. "Now?"

"Here now."

"Damn it, Jess!"

He threw up his hand in a gesture of resignation. "He took the bus in all the way from Wauwatosa this afternoon. He's been trying to call me from Joe's Tap down on the corner since five o'clock, but of course we haven't been home. He's been sitting there all night hoping to get a chance to talk to me, and he was phoning me one last time before they closed."

She was pacing. "Oh, this is great, this is just great. What is he, a dope pusher? I'll bet he's a dope pusher. A purse snatcher. He's probably a hit man for the Mob. A car thief." She faced him, disbelief and a soft anger in her voice.

"None of the above. He wrote some bad checks."

"Oh, great. We'll have a jailbird in the house."

Jesse raised himself to a sitting position with a broad grin, flapped invisible wings, and said, "Tweet tweet."

Pink began to border the freckles on her cheekbones. In spite of herself she had to grin back at him. "It's not the same. This guy's a criminal."

Adoration for her came to him in a surge of energy; that after everything she could still cling to the remnants of her country club innocence. His hands dug into her waist, and he pulled her down to the bed and rolled on top of her, covering her face with kisses. "You're right," he growled, his hands running slowly over her ribs. "You never know what a jailbird might do. Just how safe are you?" He assaulted her throat with gentle strokes of his mouth. "Locked up behind bars, all a man can think of is: woman, woman, woman! . . . Like a ravening animal! But don't worry, I'll protect you. Unless you displease me. Then I'll turn you over to him."

With the blood quickening all through her, moving to accommodate the path of his hands, she said, "Better stop making fun of me."

"All right. Because I'd rather make love to you." He kissed her probingly, arousingly, his breath falling in unsettled heating patterns on her skin. "But I can't." He sighed. "Max is about to arrive."

She squirmed regretfully from under his warm body and sat up, smoothing her hair. "We of the saner sex have names for men who inflame us to the fullness of our womanhood and leave us unsatisfied."

He sat up too, watching her movements with a lazy, appreciative smile. "Oh, yeah? What?"

"They're called jerks."

"If it's any consolation"—he skimmed a fingertip lightly down the inside of her arm—"I'm also inflamed to the fullness of my manhood."

"Really?" she said wickedly. "I thought that was a telephone pole in your pocket."

"That's it!" He swooped her back into his arms. "Back to bed with you. It drives me wild when you talk dirty." In a moment he added, "Mmm. See where flattery gets you?"

When the doorbell rang, she murmured, "Max is here" against his lips in the husky sweet tone of someone in the throes.

In the same tone he said, "Max can take a flying—"

"Sorry, Mr. Hospitality." She smiled. "I think you have to answer the door."

He stood up slowly. "You're right." His smile answered hers as he cupped her chin. "Do you think you could lie like that until I get back?"

"I don't know. This position could get kind of boring without you."

He dropped a kiss on her forehead. "You know I was kidding a minute ago. If you don't want him in the house, I can take him out someplace."

"I was kidding too—kind of. Let the poor guy in."

"Thanks. Don't come down if it makes you uncomfortable. He's a nice kid, though. I wouldn't let him anywhere near here otherwise."

She knew. Wrapped cocoonlike in a summer quilt, she listened to the murmur of voices floating up the stairs. At two forty-five, soft animated laughter from below roused her from a light sleep. They were still at it. Curiosity overcame her when sleep would not, and she pulled on cotton jeans and a white tank top with pearl embroidery and descended the stairs, rubbing her arms awake. On the bottom step she hesitated, then poked her head around the corner with a diffident "Hi!"

Jesse was stretched out on the couch. Max sat upright in the recliner, blinking at her nervously from behind wire-rimmed glasses that slipped down his thin nose as she entered. He was even smaller than her father, slender, loosely boned, and probably not a day over twenty.

"Oh! Mrs. Ludan!" He stood up in his tennis shoes, pushing his glasses back into place with his forefinger. "Did I wake you up?"

It would have taken a colder heart than hers to rebuff that guileless anxiety. "No. I thought I'd come down to say hello."

She had the strong feeling he hadn't heard a word

she'd said. He was staring at her worshipfully, in a way that she was only used to from people who were under seven and clad in tutus. Jesse was watching them both with amusement. She noticed there were no empty glasses on the tables. Trying to normalize things by slipping into the role of chipper homemaker, she said, "I'm getting myself something from the kitchen. Can I get you something, Max? A beer?" What do I bring a convict? Four Roses? Gin on the rocks?

"Uh, if it's not too much trouble," Max said, looking wistful, "I'd like herbal tea if you have it." Confidingly he added, "I don't like to put unnatural substances into my body."

She made sure to avoid Jesse's grin as she went to the kitchen, returning in five minutes carrying a teapot and three cups.

Sipping from his cup, thanking her, Max said, "This feels so good. It's the first peppermint tea I've had in months. I've only been out three days."

She could believe it. He bore the appearance of someone who'd been shot out of a cannon. It seemed hard for him to look directly into her eyes, and his hands made occasional aimless movements that conveyed a faint tinge of disorientation.

"I understand you and Jesse were in the same cell block," she said, trying to make the words *cell block* sound no more significant than if the men had been fraternity brothers.

"Yes. He kept me from going out of my skull."

Fascinated, she said, "I'd like to hear about it."

"It's a scary place." The light-colored eyes behind the glasses held ineffable sadness. "Like living at the bottom of a well. And the people—" He didn't seem to be able to go any further on the thought. "But Jesse used to think of the damnedest things to do to pass the time. I suppose he told you how he taught the whole cell block to play bridge? We held these bridge tournaments that would go on for days. Can you imagine all these unshaved tough guys in prison coveralls saying, 'Four no trump—five spades'?" His tight mouth took on a reminiscing smile. "He used to make up these games of dungeons and dragons for us too. Everyone got into it, even old Willie Smith, who was fifty-five and in for drunk and disorderly. Sometimes the guards played too."

How amazing, she thought. How like Jesse. She was suddenly glad that Max had come. She said, "He used to play with his younger brothers."

Max nodded. "That's what he told us. I—well, in prison I used to bend his ear all the time with stuff that was eating me. I guess that's why I came tonight. I needed someone to talk to. Everyone in prison's a bullshit artist—you kind of have to make yourself like that. It's a very paranoid place. But Jesse stayed a human being." He put down his teacup and stood, holding his hand out to Jesse. "Thanks. I was really desperate for someone to talk to."

Jesse stood and took his hand in a warm grip and clapped him on the shoulder. "Hey, I've been there," he said.

"You sure were," Max said. "But I'll bet you handled this better than I have."

And Jesse said, "You'd be surprised, Max. If that's what you think, you'd really be surprised."

It was too late for Max to catch a connecting bus back to his apartment, so she and Jesse walked him to the taxi stand two blocks away. There was a funny moment among the three of them when Jesse gave him a twenty to cover the cab fare and Max reimbursed him with a check and then discovered that his balance wouldn't cover it.

They waved good-bye to him and then meandered through the night hand in hand, the jazz strains from the open window of the lone remaining taxi at the stand drifting after them. Flirty breezes beckoned from the lake, and the aerated fragrance of tumbling water, and they could have turned down the block to their house but kept on, hearing the wave song swell as they neared the beach.

"Jess?"

"Hmm?"

"How many more of your friends from the cell block did you tell to call you anytime when they got out of jail?"

"I've been trying to remember." There was a smile in his voice. "I think about eight or nine."

Her moan was long suffering but humorous too, and it made him turn to look at her walking beside him, the faint light touching her blowing hair, the ivory roses in her earlobes, her white Windbreaker. Inside he was feeling a thousand dismantled pieces beginning to reconnect, as though the healing in his mind were a physical act, a body repairing itself. There was a burst of lightness within him matching the bright pattern of stars strung out above in an ebony heaven. He wanted to share the feeling with her in some way, but couldn't seem to find the right words.

On the street corner they passed a wire trash basket, and he said, "Hey!" And when she looked, he took his cigarette pack from his pocket and tossed it inside.

Then he closed his hands around her waist and swung

her lightly, gaily around in the golden cone of light from a street lamp. When she was set down, a little breathless, she said, "It helped you to help him!"

"Yes." It had. It was a blow against his own inner desolation and against the sensation of powerlessness that had taken this long to begin eroding. "That poor kid. I had all kinds of good advice for him wrapped up in neat ribbons like a May basket, about opening up again, about taking time before going back to work to relearn who you are . . . great advice. I wished I'd been there when I got out to give it to myself."

She laid her hand on his shoulder as they walked through the bluff-side park, weaving between sandboxes and horses on springs and monkey bars. Pewter light from the three-quarter moon dissolved in a mist on the horizon far out on the lake and lit the waves disintegrating against the breakwater.

They stepped onto a path that zigzagged down the bluff face to the sand at the water's edge. Walking slowly, holding hands, they negotiated the last hairpin turn of the trail, brushing aside dark whispers of windswept grass.

"I remember the day we went to court," she said. "You were Randolph Scott—quiet, but oh, so strong."

Together they stepped onto the beach, taking off their shoes, feeling the dry sand swirl like cool satin against their skin.

"No, I cried that day," he said, and experienced a burst of heady pleasure at having been able to tell her at last.

She took a quick step in front of him and laid her hands on his chest, searching his face. "When?"

He stroked her hair back from her face and gently collected it in his hands behind her neck, treasuring it away from the wanton wind. "In the property room, after I was ordered upstairs. I don't think I've told you much about that day . . ."

"No."

"The hearing was . . . something I'll never forget. Four hours. There was no kidding around, Chris. They wanted me to talk. Again and again the judge would lean over at me and say, "Are you aware, Mr. Ludan, that if you refuse to answer that question you can be charged with conspiracy and we can lock you off the streets for the next seven years of your life?' And I'd say, 'Excuse me, Your Honor, I'd like to confer with my attorney,' and I'd go back to Jack and say, 'Jesus, can they do that?' And he'd say, 'Take it easy, Jess, they can, but not without risking a national hurricane over it.' And when I said, 'Would they do that?' he said he didn't know.

"And finally Jack leaned over to me and said, 'Kid, if you don't answer them now, they're going to nail your rear end in prison.' I was sick, Chris, sick and sweating; but I heard myself refuse again and the judge whapped his gavel and said, 'Sir, you're in violation of section 972.08 of the Wisconsin state statutes and I order you confined to the county jail for a period of one year, or until such time as this investigation is concluded.' Slam. That was it. Jack asked for bail and work release. The judge denied them both."

He bent one knee forward. His brow pressed against hers. "I had that one second to tell Jack a message for you, and then the sheriff's deputy came and put cuffs on me—"

"Cuffs!" Her involuntary cry sent a stream of warm air against his lips.

"It's standard. And in the back hall they locked me

in ankle chains to these other guys who'd just been convicted."

"Oh, dear God," she whispered, her arms stretched up around his neck, clinging tightly.

"It was like becoming a subhuman form of life," he said jerkily, rubbing her with his brow. "Then they took us up to the property room and I just kept thinking, My God, a year, a year away from Christine, and I thought, What if they bring charges against me and I'm here for seven years? Seven years, Christine. What would have happened between us?" He stopped briefly to press a shaking kiss on her lips. "And then they came and put my whole identity into a brown envelope with my name on it—pens, billfold, watch, even my goddamn shoelaces—and then they wanted to take my wedding ring, and that's when I cried."

He was shaking slightly. His eyes were closed, but she could feel the curve of his cheek forming a smile.

"Can you believe it?" he said. "Of all the places to break down. No one could find any Kleenex, of course, so there I stood, snuffling into my sleeve. The guards were looking uncomfortable as hell because they don't want to have to lock up some poor loser of a reporter, and behind me this guy who'd been convicted of armed robbery patted my shoulder and asked me if it was my first time. That's why I asked you not to come, Chris. I could pretend over the phone."

The pressure of his arms on her back became almost painful, but she didn't care.

"Do you know," she said softly, tracing a finger down his cheek, "I've never seen you cry. What was it like?"

"Suffocating. I haven't had enough practice to do it properly. My body ached everywhere, as if I had the flu.

I was a real spectacle, let me tell you. What would you have thought if you'd seen me like that?"

"That you were human, Jess," she whispered. "Just that you were human."

He pulled back and looked at her, and then he kissed her in the delicate breezes of a new day.

They sat together in the sand, watching the dawn. Peachy fingers shot up from the horizon, reaching into the night's fleeing purple, reflecting on the water as it changed from black to sky blue and cloud white. The gulls wheeled and looked for nourishment, and, out at the mouth of the harbor, the breakwater was doing its job.

"I've been thinking, Jesse," she said, "about your column. I know you think that hard news is more important, but if the column goes daily, you can dig into whatever you want. Topical things too."

"True." He dragged her onto his lap, laying back the open sides of her Windbreaker. His head bent, he placed his lips on the rise of her chest above the lacy edge of her top, sensitizing himself to each breath she took.

"When I was growing up," he said softly, "I never knew it would be like this."

"What?"

"Love," he said. "I never knew it would be this deep." His hands gently swept her sides, caressing the smooth warmth beneath her breasts, and then, with his thumbs beside them, he absorbed her deepening exhalations with his mouth. "We have a lifetime to make up that six months, don't we?"

"A lifetime . . ." she said.

They helped each other to stand up and began to walk back toward the bluff, and home. Sand clung to them, and the sweet tang of sleeplessness, but in their eyes was a tender joy that no burden would ever dim. Jesse stopped halfway to the cliff and drew her against his heart. Their lips came together in a moment of clinging honey, her hair falling down his shoulders, her arms wrapped around his neck.

"We've made it, Chris," he said. "We've made it."

DON'T MISS THESE TITLES
IN THE
SECOND CHANCE AT LOVE SERIES